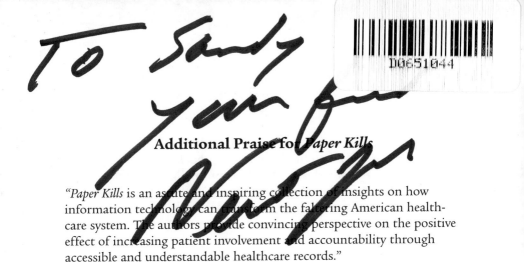

Additional Praise for *Paper Kills*

"*Paper Kills* is an astute and inspiring collection of insights on how information technology can transform the faltering American healthcare system. The authors provide convincing perspective on the positive effect of increasing patient involvement and accountability through accessible and understandable healthcare records."

    Michael Howe, CEO, MinuteClinic

"Merritt helps us to move from the horse to the automobile. If we could just close our eyes and imagine the end-game of electronic health records for all—with the vastly improved quality of care and efficiency—this book gives us a way to get there."

    Arthur Garson, Jr., M.D., M.P.H., Dean, School of Medicine, and Vice President, University of Virginia; Former Chair, Agency for Healthcare Quality and Research National Advisory Council

"Personal health records are the decade's single most important innovation for consumers to help take control of their healthcare. CHT gives us a compilation of expert opinion, practical application, and strategic thinking and offers a practical approach that will move health IT—including PHRs—into the mainstream."

    Archelle Georgiou, M.D., Executive Vice President, UnitedHealth Group

"Health information technology is an important tool to address the root problems our country faces in healthcare. IT not only improves the delivery of care, but it is essential to ridding the system of waste, be it administrative and process inefficiencies or the underuse, overuse, or misuse of medical care."

    Bruce E. Bradley, Director, Health Plan Strategy and Public Policy, General Motors Corporation

"The vision of transforming healthcare to deliver better outcomes at lower costs is clearly laid out in this important book. The realization of this vision can only come, however, by fundamentally restructuring how we pay for healthcare. The chapters in this book inspire all who are hard at work to create a payment environment that will make the vision a reality."

François de Brantes, National Coordinator, Bridges To Excellence

"*Paper Kills* creates a compelling case for healthcare industry leaders to commit to utilizing information technology tools to meet our mission of providing optimal care to those we serve. Hospital CEOs around the country should take note of this book and use it as a road map to develop a vision and strategic plan for interoperability, electronic medical records, and personal health information. Lives will be saved as a result of this book."

Marsha Burke, Interim CEO, WellStar Health System

"*Paper Kills* should be required reading for anyone interested in health-care today—from those deeply involved in both policy and operational matters to consumers trying to make sense of it all. This book lays out in clear and accessible terms the major issues in health IT and forcefully demonstrates why both increased adoption and accelerated innovation can dramatically improve healthcare in America."

The Honorable Aneesh Chopra, Virginia's Secretary of Technology and Co-Chair of the Governor's Health Information Technology Council

"*Paper Kills* is a must-read for everyone to understand that information technology can make our healthcare system safer, more efficient, and more affordable. CHT has been at the heart of this movement for years, and this book lays out how we can build a modernized system where clinicians can make life-saving decisions with accurate, updated, and complete information on the patients they treat."

Kevin Hutchinson, President and CEO, SureScripts; Member, American Health Information Community

Other Center for Health Transformation Books

The Art of Transformation by Newt Gingrich and Nancy Desmond

Making Medicaid Work by CHT and SHPS

Saving Lives & Saving Money by Newt Gingrich, with Dana Pavey
and Anne Woodbury

Available at www.healthtransformation.net

The Center for Health Transformation, founded by former U.S. House Speaker Newt Gingrich, is a high-impact collaboration of private and public sector leaders committed to creating a 21st Century Intelligent Health System that saves lives and saves money for all Americans. The Center helps create and accelerate the adoption of transformational health solutions that will give all Americans more choices of greater quality at lower cost. For more information, visit www.healthtransformation.net.

CHT Press is the publishing division of the Center for Health Transformation and was established in 2006 with the release of *The Art of Transformation*, written by Newt Gingrich and CEO Nancy Desmond.

CHT Press
1425 K Street, NW
Suite 450
Washington, D.C. 20005

President and CEO: Nancy Desmond
Media Coordinator: Megan Meehan

Internet address: www.healthtransformation.net

Additional copies of this book may be ordered by calling 202-375-2001 or visiting the CHT website at www.healthtransformation.net.

ISBN 978-1-933966-02-1

The authors, editors, and publisher of this work have checked with sources believed to be reliable in their efforts to confirm the accuracy and completeness of the information presented. However, neither the authors nor the publisher nor any party involved in the creation and publication of this work warrant that the information is in every respect accurate and complete, and they are not responsible for any errors or omissions or for any consequences from application of the information in this book.

Information provided in this book is for educational and demonstration purposes and is not intended to constitute legal advice. If legal advice is required, the services of a competent professional should be sought. All comments, opinions, and observations are those of the authors, and do not represent official positions or opinions unless specifically noted.

Paper Kills

Transforming Health and Healthcare with Information Technology

Edited by David Merritt

Brandon Savage, M.D. • Mark A. Rothstein, J.D.

W. Edward Hammond, Ph.D. • Edward Fotsch, M.D.

Richard J. Umbdenstock • Glen E. Tullman

Scott P. Serota • Thomas M. Fritz • Jac J. Davies

Mark E. Frisse, M.D. • W. Michael Heekin

Beryl L. Vallejo, Dr.P.H., R.N. • Richard Bankowitz, M.D., M.B.A., F.A.C.P.

Meg Horgan, R.N., M.S.N. • Eugene A. Kroch, Ph.D.

Published by CHT Press

Acknowledgments

Transforming health and healthcare is not possible without the dedication of forward-thinking policymakers and the innovation of private sector entrepreneurs. We at the Center for Health Transformation are honored to work closely with many of the most transformational leaders in America. Together we will undoubtedly bring about real change and build a brighter future for our country.

This book would not have been possible without the leadership, vision, and cheerful persistence of Newt Gingrich and the entire staff at the Center for Health Transformation. Special thanks go to Megan Meehan for her excellent work reviewing the manuscript, and to Nancy Desmond for her continued leadership of CHT.

Dedication

To the members of the Center for Health Transformation and
innovators across the world, who work everyday to improve
individual health, save lives, and save money.

Paper Kills

Transforming Health and Healthcare
with Information Technology

Edited by David Merritt

Meg Horgan, R.N., M.S.N., Vice President of Consulting and Customer Services, CareScience; and Eugene A. Kroch, Ph.D., Vice President and Director of Research, CareScience

Introduction

Newt Gingrich

When I wrote *Saving Lives & Saving Money* four years ago, I outlined a future in which all Americans will live active, longer, and healthier lives. This future can be achieved because the people will be at the center of a healthcare system that has been designed for them. From their doctors and hospitals to their pharmacies and insurers, every aspect of the system will be designed to maximize their health in an effective and efficient way.

In tomorrow's healthcare system, all Americans will have access to the care that they need—and everyone will have the ability to pay for it. All Americans will be empowered to make responsible and informed decisions about their own health and healthcare. Early health, prevention, and wellness will be at the core of delivery. Treatment decisions will be based on effectiveness, and reimbursement will be driven by outcomes. Consumers will own their personal data and have a right to know the cost and quality of the treatments they receive and the providers they visit. Innovation will be rapid, and the dissemination of knowledge will be secure and in real time.

All of these are fundamental changes from today's approach to healthcare. Embracing these values is absolutely necessary in order for us to build what we at the Center for Health Transformation call a 21st Century Intelligent Health System. Health information technology is the key to getting there.

I often ask people: when was the last time you took out a pen, wrote a check for cash, and handed it to a bank teller? Most young people today have no idea what "writing a check for cash" means because online banking, debit cards, and a global ATM network is the only world they've ever known. Unfortunately, that kind of technology and that kind of reality has yet to reach healthcare. And we pay a very dear price for it.

To put it simply: paper kills.

You show me a paper medical record, and I'll tell you about the 44,000 to 98,000 Americans who are killed every year by preventable medical errors. You show me a paper prescription, and I'll tell you about the more than 7,000 Americans who die every year from unnecessary medication errors. Paper processes are not solely responsible for these deaths, but they are the eroding foundation of a broken system.

Legions of experts—from scholars to practitioners to the Institute of Medicine—have repeatedly and consistently said that information technology and a modernized, interoperable health system are absolutely vital to preventing these kinds of errors and improving the delivery of care.[1] And study after study—as well as thousands of actual installations—concludes that information technology and an interoperable system will save massive amounts of money every year.[2]

To see these benefits, we must move quickly to adopt a unified set of open interoperability standards for data exchange. Open standards will lay the foundation for a nationwide health information network by allowing everyone to use common technical platforms, architectures, and vocabularies. From there, entrepreneurs will introduce a breathtaking array of solutions that can plug in to this network and share data. New technologies can run on a variety of platforms, including cell phones, monitoring devices, and the Web. These platforms will allow physicians, providers, and other stakeholders to plug in and share information, delivering better care at lower costs.

A unified set of open interoperability standards has been achieved in other industries. The creation of the Internet is a good example to highlight. In his excellent book *The World Is Flat,* Tom Friedman details how the private sector collectively agreed upon open data standards for the Internet, so that every system spoke the same language. Prior to these open standards, proprietary systems blocked the kind of collaboration and data exchange that we now take for granted. At one time you could not exchange e-mail messages with anyone who used a different kind of system with incompatible data standards. Prior to open standards like TCP/IP, HTTP, and HTML, you could not "surf the Web" as we know it, because standards varied from system to system and site to site. These islands of isolation used their own language, platforms, and applications. But over time, programmers, vendors, and solution providers worked collaboratively to develop open standards and a common communication framework. This integrated playing field gave rise to the modern Internet and all its marvels, allowing the private sector to compete on service, functionality, and quality.

That is exactly what we need in healthcare. Those physician offices, hospitals, and other sites that have been modernized through health information technology have built customized silos with invisible moats around their data, shielding it from virtually everyone. There are many reasons, ranging from competitive pressures to a lack of incentives, that only a handful of pioneers share data. But even if the majority of healthcare providers were willing to share data, the lack of consensus on open standards would make it nearly impossible.

The Health Information Technology Standards Panel (HITSP), a group charged by the federal government to develop interoperable data standards, has made great progress. However, HITSP is taking its direction from the American Health Information Community (AHIC), a political body that has tried to be all things to all people. AHIC must focus on the real-world data exchange needs of physicians and other providers, such as sharing medical summaries between a physician's office and a hospital, or sharing summary data between the six specialists the average Medicare patient sees. Furthermore, the federal process has burdensome rules regarding what it can and cannot allow, but the private sector has no such constraints. The private sector has the ability to be bold and move quickly.

The National ePrescribing Patient Safety Initiative (NEPSI) is one example. Led by Allscripts, Microsoft, WellPoint, and others, NEPSI offers safe, secure, and free electronic prescribing to every physician in the country. Another example is the collaboration between America's Health Insurance Plans and the Blue Cross and Blue Shield Association. They are creating an interoperable, payer-based personal health record (PHR), where claims data can follow consumers as they move from insurer to insurer. Once they migrate to the HITSP data standards for personal health records, allowing true interoperability among all products and PHR technologies, we will be well on our way to creating a 21st Century Intelligent Health System. We need more leadership like this.

The private sector can and must deliver new solutions to break through industry paralysis and bureaucracy at all levels. Groups like the Electronic Health Record Vendor Association, made up of leading innovators such as Siemens, GE Healthcare, and Misys, have put out road maps to interoperability, and have worked with other organizations, such as Integrating the Healthcare Enterprise, to implement these solutions. Through consultation with their clients and others, technology vendors are working together to adopt interoperable, solutions-based open standards, embed them in their new products, and, to the greatest extent possible, develop upgrades to existing programs. Some of these interoperability solutions have already been selected by HITSP and approved by AHIC. Through mutual and equitable collaboration, AHIC can work with the best of the private sector to develop bold solutions that solve the most important needs of data exchange and the most pressing problems in healthcare.

Three years ago, when David Brailer began his service as the nation's first National Coordinator of Health Information Technology, there was a real sense of hope and optimism that we as a country were coming together with a common vision. David did a magnificent job of articulating that vision and rallying industry and government around a common goal.

Now that we have embarked on the difficult journey to realize that promise, we must always keep the American people at the forefront of our thoughts.

We cannot forget that improving the lives of our fellow citizens and being responsible stewards of our tax dollars is why we are exerting this great effort in the first place. Americans are demanding a 21st Century Intelligent Health System. They could not care less which data standard will be used, or how many representatives a stakeholder has on this or that council, or which bureaucrat will be appointed. What Americans really care about is a system that saves lives and saves money—period.

On behalf of the entire nation, I make this appeal to every

stakeholder in healthcare: put the pettiness aside, focus on the common solution, and do what is right for America.

Your country is counting on you.

Newt Gingrich
May 2007

Former Speaker of the U.S. House of Representatives
Founder of the Center for Health Transformation

—⟋⟍—

[1] Institute of Medicine, Committee on Quality of Health Care in America, *Crossing the Quality Chasm: A New Health System for the 21st Century* (Washington, D.C.: National Academy Press, 2001).
[2] R. Hillestand et al., "Can Electronic Medical Record Systems Transform Health Care? Potential Health Benefits, Savings and Costs," *Health Affairs* 24, no. 5 (2005): 1103–17.

CHAPTER 1

Leveraging Information Technology to Support Early Health

Brandon Savage, M.D.

—ᴍᴍ—

Editor's Introduction

Waiting to act until a catastrophe is at your doorstep is nearly always disastrous. In the United States, vastly more money is spent on treating diseases and their acute complications than on preventing them. This is akin to a "Katrina Strategy" for health, just as the levees were for New Orleans, where prevention is both undervalued and poorly supported. Witnessing what is happening today and knowing the consequences of uncontrolled childhood obesity, teenagers with type-2 diabetes, and other undeniable trends, we know we must act now. We must create a new model, one based on early detection, prevention, and wellness. By focusing on "early health," we will provide the incentives for the adoption of new tools—such as health information technology—that will deliver better outcomes, save lives, and save money.

—ᴍᴍ—

The overarching paradox in healthcare today is that our ability to postpone or prevent death has far outstripped our ability to prevent illness in the first place. The result is a growing cadre of patients with ongoing progressive diseases requiring extensive and expensive medical management. A relatively small number of chronic conditions (including cardiovascular disease, Alzheimer's disease, diabetes, and cancer) account for approximately 78 percent of healthcare expenditures in the U.S.[1] Chronic diseases have been identified as one of the top risks for economically developed countries over the next decade.[2]

Left untreated—or with inadequate treatment—these diseases can be devastating, both physically and financially. Earlier diagnosis combined with aggressive disease management can significantly reduce the impact on both body and bank account, but the complexity of this task leaves most patients receiving less than optimal care.

We stand at a tipping point in our approach to reining in the staggering costs of progressive chronic diseases. The next breakthrough in healthcare will not be an isolated diagnostic, device, or treatment. It will be the confluence of all three—with information technology (IT) as the bridge, enabling providers to predict which patients are most likely to contract a specific illness, to diagnose the condition at an earlier stage, to tailor evidence-based care based on each patient's medical history, and to monitor outcomes at both the individual and population levels. This model of care focuses on early health, rather than late disease.

What Are Early Health Technologies?

The hallmark of early health is the ability to make early, specific diagnoses for conditions that are treatable with targeted therapies. Both parts of this equation are necessary to achieve the best outcome. Obviously, the earlier treatment begins, the less severe the disease's impact will be. What, however, is the value of early diagnosis if there is no treatment available to avoid the devastating outcome?

Fortunately, early diagnostic technologies help further the advancement of targeted treatments. In fact, many of the molecular discoveries that enable early diagnosis also form the basis for the discovery of new therapies. By providing a way to visualize the course of the disease, these discoveries can accelerate the evaluation of potential new therapies. Advanced diagnostic imaging not only allows researchers to see the results of potential new therapies earlier in the disease, but can also show efficacy (or lack thereof) much earlier in the treatment. This could reduce time to market for new effective therapies and the cost of screening out ineffective therapies.

Management of congestive heart failure (CHF) provides a comprehensive example of how early health technologies can be applied. The cost of treating CHF in the U.S. is estimated to be nearly $33 billion this year.[3] In its later stages, the disease is characterized by acute flare-ups that require frequent hospitalization. Intervention at various points in the disease cycle can effectively diminish or even prevent many negative physical and financial consequences.

One of the first steps in enabling early intervention is reducing the episodic nature of care. Numerous studies have shown that home monitoring can be effective in reducing hospitalization and improving quality of life. Markers as simple as rapid weight gain, which could be caused by a buildup of fluid in the lungs, can indicate the need for adjusting treatment—but only if that information is quickly communicated to the healthcare team. Online portals and personal health records (PHRs) enable patients to log their daily weight to be reviewed between visits by the care team.

We are learning that by the time a disease begins to cause obvious anatomic changes, it is quite late in the disease process. Diseases tend to manifest first on a molecular/cellular level, followed by physiologic changes in the way the body functions. We have already made significant advances with anatomic and physiologic diagnostics that enable us to characterize a patient's stage of CHF. Now new diagnostic technologies are emerging that may soon be able to detect changes at a cellular and molecular level associated with the early stages of progressing disease—prior to actual heart failure. This could enable the development of new treatments for CHF that can be initiated before gross symptoms are evident, averting the natural progression of an incapacitating disease.

While slowing the progression of CHF is valuable, intervening before heart damage occurs will have even greater results. For example, coronary artery disease (CAD) and acute myocardial infarction (AMI) are both major risk factors for CHF. If we consistently provide preventive care for CAD and AMI patients, this would go a long way toward avoiding CHF altogether. Over time, these efforts will be augmented both by advances in genomics that enable us to identify more risk factors, and by sophisticated IT systems that allow us to target our outreach efforts to at-risk patients.

A Proactive Approach to Disease

Effective diagnosis and treatment of acute illness can usually be accomplished once symptoms have set in. If a patient has a fever and shortness of breath, the diagnosis of pneumonia can be easily confirmed by a chest X-ray; antibiotic therapy will usually result in rapid recovery with no long-term problems.

The acute, reactive model does not work, however, for diseases that develop over long periods of time and are not easily reversed in their later stages, such as CHF, cancer, or Alzheimer's disease. Every day that the condition progresses before treatment begins raises the overall cost of therapy and erodes its chances of success. Not only is late treatment less effective, but patients also often develop new diseases as a complication of their underlying chronic disease. Patients with complex conditions often see multiple providers, resulting in fragmentation of their care and records. This lack of coordination can further prolong or exacerbate the course of the disease; in the worst case, adverse interactions between therapies ordered by different providers can cause additional harm.

Currently, therapy and diagnosis are based primarily on physiologic symptoms of a disease, resulting in a reactive and often trial-and-error approach to treatment. Early screening for certain conditions, such as cervical, breast, and colon cancers, has demonstrated significant results, but this approach has yet to be fully realized. The earlier we can detect disease and monitor treatment effectiveness, the better outcomes we can produce. For example, we now have diagnostic agents that can detect abnormal blood vessel growth in tumors. Not only could this technique detect tumors at half the size of prevailing methods, but it could also disclose at a much earlier stage whether a specific treatment regimen is working for an individual patient. In this paradigm, a woman would not have to endure months of chemotherapy only to discover that her breast cancer was not responsive to the drug. We are at the threshold of an age in which we can tailor therapies that will be effective for specific patients at an earlier stage of their diseases while minimizing side effects and complications.

However, it will take more than advanced diagnostic technology to realize the promise of early health. Much of the care provided in this country is inconsistent and unpredictable. Care practices, quality, and costs vary widely by region and provider, as documented by John Wennberg's work with the Dartmouth Health Atlas. Thus, many patients do not receive the preventive measures necessary to avert suffering and cost, and basic care decisions often deviate from the latest scientific evidence. Yet there exist comprehensive evidence-based guidelines for treating many diseases, and we are at the cusp of mastering techniques that can identify an individual patient's predisposition for a specific illness. What is missing is an effective way to manage these vast sources of information and promote the necessary caregiver collaboration that will allow us to both provide more personalized, proactive care and to better manage disease across entire populations.

IT can provide the infrastructure that will enable providers to make the promise of early health a reality, to prevent suffering, and to reduce the cost of treating the plagues of acute and chronic diseases. This new paradigm of information goes beyond the static records and flowcharts we use today, creating a dynamic foundation in which evidence-based best practices can be applied to a patient's medical history (and, ultimately, genetic make-up) to establish consistent practice tailored to a patient's specific needs.

Three Ways Information Technology Supports Early Health

1. Consistent information lays the foundation for consistent care
Here we must distinguish individualized care from the inconsistencies in practice that exist today. From institution to institution, within a single organization, and even within the experience of a single provider, there are unintentional variations that do not benefit the patient. In fact, these variations produce an unreliable baseline from which to extrapolate effective innovation or personalization of care.

IT increases consistency by providing tools that support the three core processes of care: information review, documentation, and ordering.

The quality of diagnosis and treatment decisions depends on access to accurate information, including a comprehensive medical history and a reliable medical knowledge base. As care for complex diseases is increasingly handled by interdisciplinary care teams—which may include specialists in different parts of the country or even in different countries—IT is the only way every provider can access and add to the patient's complete and up-to-date medical record. The electronic health record (EHR) will be the single source for patient data, seamlessly integrating text and images.

Increasingly, EHRs will provide more than information about the patient's history and current care; they will include risk factors such as family history, long-term complications of disease, and genetic predisposition. This functionality will be further enhanced by providing caregivers with detailed information to monitor diseases and therapies at the cellular and molecular level for individual patients.

As providers review a patient's information, they transform their observations into documentation that becomes part of the medical record. Electronic documentation templates provide a consistent guide for information collected during each patient encounter, so that all relevant data will be available to the rest of the care team. Increasingly, the documentation process will be integrated with a medical knowledge base, so that providers will have immediate access to the most up-to-date information about specific medical conditions.

Physician orders represent the point at which all of this information is translated into specific recommendations to improve a patient's health. By grouping orders together into order sets, it becomes easier for providers to consistently select the best treatment for a given patient without being subject to the limitations of "cookbook" medicine. Order sets also enable healthcare organizations to effect consistent practice across the institution.

2. Embedding evidence in a personalized care infrastructure

Once there is a consistent standard for information collected about a patient, the next step is to integrate evidence-based best practice guidelines directly into the clinician's workflow using the clinical information system. At the most basic level, this means embedding guidelines that provide standardized protocols for treating specific conditions; e.g., the American Heart Association's published guidelines recommend that all heart attack patients should receive ACE inhibitors and beta blockers prior to discharge. With greater sophistication, the systems can help clinicians manage complicated care processes such as weaning a patient from a ventilator or managing a chronic disease over a long period of time. In addition, the IT system acts as a contributing member of the care team, interacting with each clinician to make sure he or she is aware of the most recent information about the patient, the most current medical knowledge about the patient's condition, and each provider's responsibilities with respect to the patient.

No provider can realistically be expected to assimilate and remember the vast quantities of ever-changing medical knowledge about even a single chronic condition, let alone all the individual variations that patients present. Clinical decision-support systems are effective because they tie medical knowledge bases, early diagnostics, preventive measures, and targeted therapies directly into the provider's workflow.

Moreover, the dynamic nature of the system means that the patient can always receive the benefit of the most current information. If research uncovers a marker that can predict a rare form of cancer, the system can notify providers of all their patients with a family history of the disease and recommend appropriate screening. Similarly, as more effective therapies are developed for specific conditions, the system can notify providers about the new protocols and compile a list of those patients most likely to benefit from them. As a result, the adoption of early health technologies can be greatly accelerated.

Intermountain Healthcare in Salt Lake City, Utah, is one of the nation's leaders in outcomes-based care. Not coincidentally, based on a study of outcomes data for Medicare patients with chronic illness, Intermountain provides higher quality care for about one-third less cost than most other healthcare organizations nationwide.[4] It achieves this in part by assisting clinicians to practice evidence-based medicine. That is, all processes of delivering care are designed according to what works and what does not. This is done by combining clinical best practices and expert processes with computer-based decision support that incorporates data from the patient's medical record.

For example, heart attack patients can often benefit from medications such as statins to lower cholesterol and beta blockers to reduce the load on the heart, making it easier for the damaged heart to do its work and reduce the potential impact of CHF. Yet at many healthcare organizations, patients are sent home without the appropriate prescriptions.

After Intermountain introduced computer alerts to prompt clinicians about these medications prior to a patient's discharge from the hospital, the institution saw dramatic results. In the first year, the protocol:

- prevented 551 readmissions for CHF

- saved $2.5 million because of the reduced readmissions
- prevented 331 deaths from complications of CHF

Localization of protocols is another way in which care can be tailored, in this case to populations rather than individuals. One of the criticisms of evidence-based care is that the results may not be appropriate to a given provider's patient population. IT can overcome this objection by turning that population into a living clinical trial. Aggregating information on the outcomes of specific practices into a data warehouse allows analysis of the impact on that population. The results can be used to modify existing practices as indicated by the population-specific data. At a macro level, IT can accelerate the process of making these population-specific modifications.

3. IT enables collaboration to maximize value

The third way in which IT supports early health is by promoting active collaboration across the traditional boundaries of time, location, discipline, and specialty.

Healthcare delivery today continues to be episodic and fragmented in nature, largely because of the difficulty in sharing information even within a single organization. Without a more integrated view of a patient's history and condition, it is virtually impossible to ensure that patients receive the highest-quality, most efficient care.

To achieve early health, providers will need to be able to collaborate more effectively, each playing the appropriate role at the appropriate time, as dictated by the patient's condition. The amount of information to be integrated and the number of interactions to be coordinated for this effort is massive. IT is needed to facilitate a shared story of care, so that management of the disease can be actively coordinated and optimized across all providers.

Collaboration can be extended to the patient through a personal health record, making the patient an important part of the care process. Patients can provide more frequent observations about their disease state, which can be stored separately from the official medical record but dynamically integrated as needed for care decisions. In this way, patients are empowered to become more involved in their own care. The more knowledge patients have about their conditions, the better able they are to make appropriate decisions for their care outside a healthcare organization.

Managing Population Health

Currently, our system of healthcare delivery depends on patients to initiate efforts for a health intervention or care that can prevent or improve the course of a disease. Unfortunately, most patients do not know when they should ask for such support. Population management enables healthcare organizations to proactively identify those patients who can benefit from early health and encourage them to engage in preventive care.

PeaceHealth, an integrated delivery network with six acute care hospitals and multiple physician clinics in the Pacific Northwest, mines the data in its electronic health system to view key health indicators for all its patients. The organization can compare this data against national benchmarks, and can even analyze performance by region, by clinic, or even by a single provider.

PeaceHealth couples this population-based disease management approach with aggressive individualized disease management to achieve significant improvement in the key indicators it tracks. For example, in 2002, 36 percent of patients registered LDL cholesterol levels lower than 100 (the target for optimum health). By 2006, 51 percent had LDL levels at or below 100. And the number of patients with hemoglobin A1C levels less than seven has increased from 45 percent in 2002 to 54 percent in the years since. Studies show that keeping A1C levels low decreases the risk of blindness, kidney failure, heart attack, and other microvascular complications.

Population management can become even more powerful as electronic health records are able to capture the inherent risks of certain diseases among groups of patients. For example, by analyzing the varying risk profiles in a population, a health system can reach out proactively to groups at risk for heart disease, cancers, stroke, and other life-threatening conditions and provide them with tailored plans for health and disease prevention.

While many of the advances of early health are being driven by technical and scientific developments today, it will take an unprecedented paradigm shift across the research, provider, and vendor communities to reshape our healthcare model into one that truly is as preventive as possible. By combining clinical knowledge and advanced technologies, we can take a quantum leap in how we prevent, diagnose, and treat some of the deadliest, costliest, and most pervasive diseases—and ultimately change healthcare as we know it.

—⚭—

Brandon Savage, M.D., is Chief Medical Officer and General Manager of Global Marketing for GE Healthcare's Integrated IT Solutions business. His responsibilities include working with the healthcare community to establish GE's healthcare IT vision and driving requirements into current and future products that enable digital communities and early health. At GE, Dr. Savage has led the development of products such as computerized provider order entry (CPOE) and other software applications focused on knowledge management, collaborative workflow, and decision support. Prior to joining GE, Dr. Savage practiced internal medicine and was an assistant professor of medicine at the University of California–San Diego with a focus on clinical trials and patient safety. He also co-founded Intensive Solutions International, which developed software for managing patients in intensive care units.

—⚭—

[1] G. Anderson and J. Horvath, "The Growing Burden of Chronic Disease in America," *Public Health Reports* 119, no. 3 (2004): 263–70.

[2] World Economic Forum, *Global Risks 2007: A Global Risk Network Report,* January 2007. Available at http://www.weforum.org/pdf/CSI/Global_Risks_2007.pdf (accessed April 6, 2007).

[3] American Heart Association, Statistics Committee and Stroke Statistics Subcommittee, "Heart Disease and Stroke Statistics: 2007 Update," *Circulation,* December 28, 2006. Available at http://circ.ahajournals.org/cgi/content/short/CIR-CULATIONAHA.106.179918 (accessed March 23, 2007).

[4] Dartmouth Atlas Project, *The Care of Patients with Severe Chronic Illness: An Online Report on the Medicare Program,* 2006. Available at http://www.dartmouthatlas.org/atlases/2006_Chronic_Care_Atlas.pdf (accessed April 6, 2007).

CHAPTER 2

Protecting Privacy and Confidentiality in the Nationwide Health Information Network

Mark A. Rothstein, J.D.*

—⚭—

Editor's Introduction

Information about our health and healthcare is by far the most sensitive data we own. From chronic conditions to medications to genetic makeup, our personal health information reveals intimate details about who we are, what we do, and what we may be like in the future. Thus, protecting our privacy and confidentiality is a principle that simply cannot be compromised. As the pace of modernizing healthcare quickens through health information technology, tension grows between protecting patients' personal data and having instant access to their comprehensive medical histories. On the one hand, having real-time access to personal health information—such as current medications and allergies—can often mean the difference between life and death. On the other hand, the release of such sensitive data to outsiders, especially those with nefarious or self-interested intentions, can have disastrous consequences. An interoperable, nationwide system will undoubtedly save lives and save money, and it is an absolutely essential part of transforming health. But it must be built, deployed, and adopted in a manner that ensures responsible, appropriate, and authorized use.

—⚭—

Privacy, including health privacy, is an intriguing concept. In the United States, virtually everyone is in favor of health privacy. But when people are confronted with the costs it entails—in inconvenience and expense—the public's support for it declines. Furthermore, there is no generally accepted definition of what health privacy actually means. For instance, the primary privacy concerns of the public

---

* Mr. Rothstein serves as Chair of the Subcommittee on Privacy and Confidentiality of the National Committee on Vital and Health Statistics, the federal advisory committee charged with advising the Secretary of Health and Human Services on health information policy. The views expressed in this chapter, however, are solely those of the author.

regarding adoption of electronic health records (EHRs) are that irresponsible healthcare entities and rogue employees will divulge information or that snoops and hackers will get access to private information,[1] but these concerns are more properly characterized as health information security issues.

The definition of health privacy comprises at least the following four meanings: (1) informational privacy, which concerns access to personal information; (2) physical privacy, which concerns access to persons and personal spaces; (3) decisional privacy, which concerns governmental and other third-party interference with personal choices; and (4) proprietary privacy, which concerns the appropriation and ownership of interests in human personality.[2]

Confidentiality is closely related to privacy. It refers to the conditions surrounding a situation when information provided within a confidential relationship (e.g., physician-patient) may be disclosed to others. Confidentiality has been a cardinal principle of medical ethics since the time of Hippocrates. With confidentiality, physicians offer their patients the following arrangement: accept a lower level of control over your sensitive health information (confidentiality vs. nondisclosure), because doing so is important to your health, and your information will not be disclosed without your permission.

Privacy and confidentiality are sometimes viewed as individual rights that clash with the societal interest of disclosure of health information. In fact, society has a strong interest in protecting privacy and confidentiality because public health would be endangered if people were afraid to share sensitive information with their healthcare providers. At the same time, individuals have a strong interest in disclosure, because medical research and other social goods depend on the availability of individual health information. Thus, the costs and benefits of privacy and confidentiality need to be balanced for the benefit of both individuals and society.

The development of the Nationwide Health Information Network (NHIN) raises important questions of privacy and confidentiality. As the amount of easily accessible health information increases, so too do the potential risks to privacy and confidentiality stemming from inappropriate disclosures. Consequently, unless the public is satisfied that adequate measures are in place to protect health information, the political viability of the NHIN will be threatened.[3]

Today's Protections for Health Privacy and Confidentiality

America's healthcare system protects privacy and confidentiality in three ways. First, confidentiality is a basic element of medical ethics. In 1847, the first Code of Ethics of the American Medical Association (AMA) expressly recognized the importance of confidentiality,[4] and all subsequent versions of the AMA Code, as well as the ethical codes of nurses, dentists, pharmacists, and other health professionals, recognize the importance of confidentiality.[5] Regardless of legal protections or health information technology, confidentiality is, in the first instance, based on the integrity and professional ethics of those who use health information in providing care.

Second, health privacy and confidentiality are protected by a patchwork of federal and state laws. The Health Insurance Portability and Accountability Act (HIPAA) Privacy Rule[6] is the closest thing to a comprehensive health privacy law, but it has limited coverage. The privacy provisions are part of a federal law addressing health claims, and therefore they apply only to health providers, health plans, and health clearinghouses that submit or pay health claims in standard electronic formats. Thus, HIPAA does not apply to employers, schools, life insurers, and other entities that routinely access, use, and disclose health information. Nor does it apply to the myriad providers who do not submit claims in electronic form. Information protected while under the custody of a covered entity loses its protected status when it is disclosed to a non-covered entity. Furthermore, there are few limits on the re-disclosure of health information to "business associates" of covered entities, including those located off-shore.

Other federal laws have even more limited applicability. For example, the federal Privacy Act[7] applies only to health information in the possession of the federal government. Another law protects the confidentiality of substance abuse treatment information,[8] so that illicit drug users (who are breaking the law) will seek treatment without fear of arrest. The Americans with Disabilities Act limits the types of health record disclosures permissible in the employment setting.[9] Other laws deal with health information in biomedical research.[10]

Several states have laws setting forth privacy and confidentiality rules for healthcare, such as the need for patient consent for disclosure of information.[11] Many states also have laws applicable to certain types of information, such as mental health records, genetic information and HIV/AIDS status. These laws attempt to protect what is perceived to be some of the most sensitive or stigmatizing information.

The third factor protecting the confidentiality of health information is the fragmentation of our largely paper-based health records system. As a practical matter, it would be virtually impossible to identify and aggregate all an individual's medical records, which might be stored in dozens of physicians' offices, hospitals, laboratories, and other facilities in diverse locations. Consequently, individuals can be fairly certain that the otherwise lamentable lack of coordination of their health information has the indirect effect of protecting from disclosure disparate health records that could contain sensitive information. This inadvertent protection, however, is likely to disappear with the creation of the NHIN.

Patients' Rights

A health records system that respects privacy and confidentiality should empower individuals to take an active role in deciding the proper use and disclosure of their health information. To accommodate wide choices for patients, a health record system must be flexible; but if patients have too much control over the content of health records, the records might be inadequate to provide essential information for healthcare. Thus, recognizing the importance of meaningful patient choice over aspects of their health records should not be seen as endorsing unlimited patient control.

The Right to Accept or Decline Participation in the Nationwide Health Information Network (NHIN)

The precise structure and operating mechanism of the NHIN have yet to be determined. Under any likely arrangement, however, individual electronic health records will be accessible via an interoperable network. At the very least, individuals should have the choice whether to make their health records available via the NHIN. It is not entirely clear what such a decision would mean in practical terms. For example, would it still permit the individual to elect, on a one-time basis, to send a particular set of medical records over the NHIN? If so, then the difference between individuals whose records may be sent "automatically" over the NHIN and those whose records require a special, one-time authorization may be slight. To protect themselves, healthcare providers might require individual authorizations for each non-emergency use of the NHIN for all of their patients. The effect would be to turn all patients into potential one-time users, albeit at a high administrative cost.

The choice to participate in the NHIN is only a starting point. How are such decisions to be made? The most common way of framing the issue is to ask whether the system should be "opt-in" or "opt-out." In the former situation, the presumption or default is that individuals are not part of the NHIN until some express action is taken to permit disclosure. In the latter, individuals could elect not to be a part of the system, but if they do nothing, their records would be accessible via the NHIN.

Although I support the opt-in approach because it is consistent with numerous other aspects of informed consent in healthcare, in practice, there may be little difference between opt-in and opt-out. An analogous debate arose and continues to exist over the HIPAA Privacy Rule. The original proposed rule required that individuals consent to have their protected health information used and disclosed for treatment, payment, and healthcare operations.[12] The final, revised rule withdrew the requirement of consent; instead, it simply mandates that all covered entities provide a notice of privacy practices to individuals, and covered entities with a direct treatment relationship must make a good faith effort to obtain a signed acknowledgment from the individual of receipt of the notice.[13] In practice, patients are usually asked to sign the acknowledgment without any explanation of what it is and often without even receiving the notice. In this environment, replacing the acknowledgment with a consent form would make no difference to most patients, as they would merely be asked to sign a different HIPAA form, with no further explanation.

Based on the unsatisfactory experience with the HIPAA Privacy Rule's approach to notices and acknowledgments, it is imperative that executing an NHIN opt-in or opt-out document be more meaningful. Patients need understandable, culturally appropriate information about the significance of their choices. Because settings such as a hospital admissions desk and a physician's office reception area are not the best educational environments, broader public education is needed. No such program was ever implemented for the Privacy Rule, and the experience strongly suggests that unless the NHIN contains a substantial educational component, any process whereby patients indicate their decision about participating in it is likely to be deeply flawed.

The Right to Control the Contents of Records Disclosed via the NHIN

Many (or perhaps most) people are not bothered by the release of "routine" elements of their health records. They are only troubled by the prospect of disclosing the most sensitive material. For example, one study at a major medical center involved 100 individuals from each of the following six disease groups: cystic fibrosis, sickle cell disease, diabetes, HIV infection, breast cancer, and colon cancer.[14] When asked whether special privacy protections should be in place for certain medical conditions, they indicated the following conditions as most in need of special protection (in order of need): abortion history, mental health history, HIV/AIDS, genetic test results, drug/alcohol history, and sexually transmitted disease. Assuming that individuals have the right to choose whether to have their records disclosed via the NHIN, if they lack the ability to designate certain information for nondisclosure, then they will simply decline to be part of the NHIN. Thus, some degree of specificity regarding the records to be disclosed is essential to maximize participation in the NHIN.

It may be difficult to determine the appropriate level of patient control over their health records. If patients have too little control, they might decline to have their records accessible via the NHIN; but giving them too much control might not be a good idea, either. For example, if patients had the right to select *any* items in their health records for nondisclosure via the NHIN, then healthcare providers receiving the records would be unsure as to what items could have been removed. To be safe, many providers might obtain a complete medical history for each new patient, thereby eliminating a primary benefit of the NHIN.

One way of giving patients an appropriate degree of control over their information disclosed via the NHIN would be to establish standard information fields that could be selected by patients for nondisclosure. Such criteria might be based on the age of the information (e.g., items over ten years old), the type of information (e.g., mental health, substance abuse), the type of provider (e.g., psychiatrist), or other bases. If both patients and providers know the rules of disclosure, then privacy could be protected without the need for taking new comprehensive histories. Physicians might inquire, for example, if information from an "optional" field might affect diagnosis or treatment.

One strategy for implementing the approach of selective nondisclosure is the use of "blocking." Patients could designate certain areas of their records to be blocked from disclosure to all or a subset of their healthcare providers. Nevertheless, even if information is blocked, computerized decision support could still scan blocked information to protect patient safety.

If a patient, for example, is taking medication for a psychiatric condition, and the diagnosis and medication are blocked, the decision support would still check for a possible drug interaction between the blocked medication and a new medication under consideration by the physician. If so, then the physician would receive a message about a drug interaction with a blocked prescription. The physician then could prescribe another medication, obtain information from the patient about the blocked medication, or take other steps. Blocking with decision support is likely to improve patient safety over current prescribing practices, wherein patients often get a second prescription without mentioning the first prescription to their physician.

The Right to Control the Contents of Local Health Records
Focusing attention exclusively on health records as they are transmitted via the NHIN is too narrow. For one thing, in the architecture of the NHIN (or some future version of it), any distinctions between "local" records and "network" records may dissipate. Second, patients may not recognize a distinction between the two aspects of their health records. Thus, the question arises as to whether patient controls over health records should apply to local health records and, if so, how should it be done.

I see no reason why patients should not be able to control aspects of their health records regardless of the location or designation of the status of the records. The privacy interests of patients are the same, and the practicalities are often the same. For example, in a large, integrated health delivery system, the scope of actual or potential disclosures within the system (not using the NHIN) will exceed the disclosures made via the NHIN from a sole provider to another sole provider.

One way to reduce the scope of disclosure is the use of role-based access criteria, under which the level of access of any healthcare provider within a healthcare institution depends on the role and needs of the individual. Thus, treating physicians and nurses would get a higher level of access than billing clerks and food service workers. Role-based access criteria already have been adopted by many large healthcare organizations with EHR systems, and this requirement should be expressly mandated for all healthcare records systems.

An extremely contentious issue involves destruction of sensitive health records. Should individuals have the right to delete certain information from their files? As noted earlier, in a largely paper-based system, individual privacy with regard to old, sensitive health information is protected because the records tend to "disappear" with age—based on patient relocation, provider retirement, storage issues, or similar factors. In an age of electronic health records, nothing will disappear, and the protections of blocking, role-based access, or other measures will not necessarily relieve the anxiety of individuals who know that embarrassing information is in their health records.

Some physicians strongly object to the concept of patients deleting certain aspects of their medical records and assert that doing so would be unethical, illegal, or would jeopardize patient care. All these arguments are related, but none are persuasive. To begin with, medical records are obtained and retained for the benefit of the patient, and laws or professional standards limiting alteration or destruction of records are for the benefit of the patient. The AMA Code of Medical Ethics provides:

> Physicians have an obligation to retain patient records which may reasonably be of value to a patient. . . .Medical considerations are the primary basis for deciding how long to retain medical records. For example, operative notes and chemotherapy records should always be part of the patient's chart. In deciding whether to keep certain parts of the record, an appropriate

criterion is whether a physician would want the information if he or she were seeing the patient for the first time.[15]

This provision is instructive because it indicates that it is permissible for certain parts of a patient's record to be destroyed, that medical considerations govern how long records information should be kept, and that benefit to the patient is the overriding purpose of maintaining the records.

There are many examples of sensitive health information in medical files with no continued clinical relevance. Here are two examples:

(1) A 25-year-old woman comes to the emergency department of a local hospital with bruises and minor lacerations as a result of being abused by her boyfriend. She is treated and released. She promptly breaks up with her boyfriend. Twenty years later, she is happily married to another man and has two healthy children. Does her report of abuse at the hands of her old boyfriend need to remain in her file?

(2) A 25-year-old graduate student celebrates the end of exams with an evening of excessive drinking and carousing, which ends with a liaison with a commercial sex worker. A week later, concerned about the health implications of the adventure, he has his physician run a battery of tests for sexually transmitted diseases. All the tests are negative and the carousing is not repeated. Does the record of sexually transmitted disease testing, and the reason for it, need to remain in his file for the rest of his life?

I would argue that deleting sensitive health information under some appropriate standards and procedures would be ethical, not jeopardize patient health, and would support public health by not discouraging individuals from seeking care in sensitive situations. To the extent that removing certain information is unlawful, which the AMA asserts is not usually the case,[16] applicable laws should be amended or repealed.

The Right to Know Disclosures Beyond Healthcare
The loss of health privacy creates a substantial risk of tangible harm to individuals. Ironically, the disclosures leading to these harms are almost always lawful. In the United States, laws to protect health

privacy are designed to protect against unauthorized access to, use of, and disclosure of personal health information. Few laws place any restrictions on the scope of information that third parties may require individuals to disclose pursuant to an authorization. Individuals need not sign an authorization to release their health records, but if they refuse, they will not be considered for employment, life insurance, or other essential transactions or opportunities. Furthermore, disclosures of health records pursuant to an authorization tend to comprise the entire record, regardless of any limitations listed in the authorization.

Few people realize the pervasiveness of compelled authorizations. In a recent article, Meghan Talbott and I estimated the number of compelled authorizations each year in the United States at 25 million.[17] The list of uses includes health information disclosed for employment entrance examinations, individual health insurance applications, individual life insurance applications, individual long-term care insurance applications, individual disability insurance applications, individual and group disability insurance claims, automobile insurance personal injury claims, Social Security Disability Insurance applications, workers' compensation claims, veterans' disability claims, and personal injury lawsuits. It is impossible to protect health privacy and confidentiality without regulating compelled disclosures of health information.

Although it is often necessary for third parties to consider an individual's health information in each of the uses described above, it is rarely necessary to consider an individual's entire health record. Moreover, with the advent of the NHIN, the amount of information accessible about each individual will increase dramatically. Thus, it is likely that more sensitive health information of no relevance to a non-healthcare use might be routinely disclosed millions of times each year.

Contextual access criteria are computer software programs or algorithms that enable the holders of health information to limit the scope of the disclosures.[18] For example, using this technique, life insurance companies would receive only information related to mortality risk and employers would receive only information related to the individual's ability to perform a specific job. It will be a challenge to develop the criteria for each of the common, non-medical uses of health information and then to develop the programs to isolate these data fields in electronic health records. It will also be a challenge to garner the political support to restrict the scope of disclosures. Nevertheless, research efforts to develop the technology of contextual access criteria must be undertaken immediately. If the NHIN goes forward without the architecture to support contextual access criteria, it may be impossible or prohibitively expensive to add this feature later.

Nonclinical Uses of the NHIN

A network of interoperable, longitudinal, comprehensive EHRs has many potential applications beyond promoting efficient, effective, and safe clinical care for individuals. The data derived from aggregation of individual health information would provide a rich resource for epidemiology, outcomes research, population health statistics, health quality research, healthcare utilization review, and fraud investigation. Currently, the most aggressive non-clinical use of the NHIN being developed is for real-time biosurveillance, involving natural (e.g., influenza) and man-made (e.g., bioterrorism) health threats.

Although national security is an area of great public concern, using biosurveillance as a prominent initial application of the NHIN raises significant issues. Even if privacy and confidentiality were well protected in a biosurveillance system, an emphasis on this issue might lead members of the public to question the veracity of official pronouncements that the NHIN is being created primarily to improve personal health. Before establishing a national biosurveillance system using the NHIN, five considerations need to be addressed and satisfactorily resolved.

First, public officials need to make a compelling case regarding both the need for and efficacy of such a new system. Pilot projects and smaller start-up measures should be undertaken before the NHIN is used.

Second, the measures used by the system should be the least intrusive possible. The minimum amount of data should be released to the fewest number of people in the least identifiable form.

Third, there should be transparency in establishing the system, and all stakeholders (e.g., state and local public health officials, healthcare providers, members of the public) should have an opportunity to participate in its design. To date, there has been little notice and even less public participation.

Fourth, public and professional education about the objectives, operations, and safeguards of the system is essential.

Fifth, there should be an ongoing program of independent oversight, assessment, and research to ascertain whether the system is meeting its goals and adequately protecting privacy and confidentiality.

Conclusion

The NHIN is different from other large health database projects because it is intended to facilitate the dissemination of clinical data. The participants in the NHIN are not volunteer research subjects. They are patients in clinical settings who have done nothing to enroll in the NHIN except to enter the healthcare system.

Given this framework, it is clear that the developers of the NHIN have a substantial ethical responsibility not to harm the interests of patients, and to protect their privacy and confidentiality. The interests of patients must take precedence over other intended uses of the system. There must be public participation in the system's design and a well-financed, vigorous public education program before the NHIN goes into effect. Fair information practices, such as accounting for disclosures and a complaint resolution process, should be incorporated into the NHIN. Individuals should have the right to choose whether to participate and, if they do, they should have some control over the content of the health information disclosed. Contextual access criteria to limit the scope of information disclosed to third parties for non-medical purposes should be part of the architecture of the NHIN. Strong enforcement is needed and there should be an ongoing program of research to assess the effects of the NHIN and its privacy measures.

If the preceding list seems long, difficult, and expensive—it is. Privacy and confidentiality are not cheap, and they are not easy. These protections, however, are crucial in establishing and maintaining public trust in the NHIN and its component parts. To do less would risk losing public confidence in the entire healthcare system and exposing individuals to a range of tangible and intangible harms.

—⁑—

Mark A. Rothstein, J.D., holds the Herbert F. Boehl Chair of Law and Medicine and is Director of the Institute for Bioethics, Health Policy, and Law at the University of Louisville School of Medicine. Professor Rothstein is a leading authority on the ethical, legal, and social implications of genetics, privacy, occupational health, employment law, and public health law. He is Chair of the Subcommittee on Privacy and Confidentiality of the National Committee on Vital and Health Statistics, the statutory advisory committee to the Secretary of Health and Human Services on health information policy, including the privacy regulations of the Health Insurance Portability and Accountability Act. He is the immediate past President of the American Society of Law, Medicine and Ethics. He is the author or editor of 19 books. His latest book is entitled *Genetics: Ethics, Law and Policy*. He received his B.A. from the University of Pittsburgh and his J.D. from Georgetown University.

—⁑—

[1] Harris Interactive, "Health Information Privacy (HIPAA) Notices Have Improved Public's Confidence That Their Medical Information Is Being Handled Properly," news release, February 24, 2005. Available at http://www.harrisinteractive.com/news/allnewsbydate.asp?NewsID=893 (accessed March 30, 2007).

[2] Anita L. Allen, "Genetic Privacy: Emerging Concepts and Values," in *Genetic Secrets: Protecting Privacy and Confidentiality in the Genetic Era,* ed. Mark A. Rothstein (New Haven, CT: Yale University Press, 1997), 31–59.

[3] National Committee on Vital and Health Statistics, Letter to Health and Human Services Secretary Mike Leavitt, June 26, 2006. Available at http://www.ncvhs.hhs.gov/060622lt.htm (accessed March 23, 2007).

[4] American Medical Association, *Code of Medical Ethics of the American Medical Association,* art. I, § 2, 93 (1847). Available at http://www.ama-assn.org/ama/upload/mm/369/1847code.pdf (accessed March 30, 2007).

[5] Rena A. Gorlin, ed., *Codes of Professional Responsibility: Standards in Business, Health and Law,* 4th ed. (Washington, D.C.: BNA Books, 1999).

[6] 45 C.F.R. Parts 160, 164 (2004).

[7] 5 U.S.C. § 552a (2000).

[8] 42 C.F.R. Part 2 (2004).

[9] 42 U.S.C. § 12112(d) (2000).

[10] 45 C.F.R. Part 46 (2004).

[11] Joy Pritts et al., *The State of Health Policy: A Survey of State Health Privacy Statutes,* 2nd ed. (Washington, D.C.: Georgetown University Press, 2002). Available at

http://hpi.georgetown.edu/privacy/pdfs/statereport1.pdf (accessed March 30, 2007).

[12] Department of Health and Human Services, "Standards for Privacy of Individually Identifiable Health Information," *Federal Register* 65, no. 250 (December 28, 2000): 82,462-829 (proposed section 164.506(a)).

[13] 45 C.F.R. § 164.520 (c)(2)(ii).

[14] Laura Plantinga et al., "Disclosure, Confidentiality, and Families: Experiences and Attitudes of Those With Genetic versus Nongenetic Medical Conditions," *American Journal of Medical Genetics* 119C, no. 1 (2003): 51.

[15] American Medical Association, Code of Medical Ethics § 7.05: Retention of Medical Records (2006-2007 ed.) (2006).

[16] Ibid.

[17] Mark A. Rothstein and Meghan K. Talbott, "Compelled Authorizations for Disclosures of Health Records: Magnitude and Implications," *American Journal of Bioethics* 7, no. 3 (2007): 38-45.

[18] Mark A. Rothstein and Meghan K. Talbott, "Compelled Disclosures of Health Information: Protecting against the Greatest Potential Threat to Privacy," *Journal of the American Medical Association* 295 (2006): 2882-85.

CHAPTER 3

Solving the Interoperability Dilemma

W. Edward Hammond, Ph.D.

—⟋⟍—

Editor's Introduction

There will be no Nationwide Health Information Network without interoperability. There will be no life-saving, real-time access to critical patient information without interoperability. There will be no true consumer ownership of personal health information without interoperability. And that is merely the beginning. Interoperability is the key to a different future in health, one in which every American can get better health at lower costs. Examples abound of other industries and organizations overcoming the hurdles of competition, self-interest, and distrust to create seamless networks of communication. The stakeholders in healthcare must do the same. An individual company may wonder why it would ever embrace a future in which its data can easily flow from one system to another—and from one competitor to another. In fact, it is not rational to embrace interoperability if you view it from this perspective, as many organizations profit from today's inefficiencies. But when viewed from a comprehensive and system-wide perspective, eschewing interoperability in favor of today's world of isolated silos is utterly irrational. We must do what is right for our country—and not necessarily our immediate bottom lines—and build a brighter future for America.

—⟋⟍—

"Interoperability" has become the most important term in health information technology. It is important because of the need, driven by many factors, to merge individual patient data from the many sites where patients receive care and then share that data appropriately with other participants within the system. In short, interoperability means connecting every healthcare provider and every appropriate piece of patient information for use at the point of care. The sharing of this interoperable data will create a comprehensive patient-centric electronic health record (EHR) and will allow researchers and caregivers to analyze aggregated data that will undoubtedly lead to better care.

Consensus plays a significant role in achieving interoperability, and it is critical to note that there is no consistent definition of interoperability or view of what is required to achieve it. A widely accepted definition for interoperability comes from the Institute of Electrical and Electronic Engineers (IEEE): "Interoperability is the ability of two or more systems or components to exchange information and to use that information that has been exchanged."[1] The National Alliance for Health Information Technology (NAHIT) defines interoperability as "the ability of different information technology systems, software applications, and networks to communicate, to exchange data accurately, effectively, and consistently, and to use the information that has been exchanged."[2] Dr. David Brailer, former head of the Office of the National Coordinator for Health Information Technology, defines interoperability as "a seamless flow of patient information as specified by the patient or by the physician." With these various definitions, clearly defining true interoperability and how to accomplish it is vital.

A Vision of True Interoperability

True interoperability is an absolute. It has no degrees or levels—an entity is either interoperable or it is not. Interoperability has many requirements, and all must be satisfied at every step of the process. Interoperability must exist across the healthcare system, starting with the smallest component and existing through the most complex application. It must exist both at the data level and at the application level. The ability to exchange information is called *functional interoperability*, and the ability to use that information is known as *semantic interoperability*. There also must be *business interoperability*, in which facilities interchanging data understand what data is to be exchanged and what triggers the exchange. With true interoperability, actions such as mapping and harmonization are not required.

The Institute of Medicine reported that a patient's electronic health record available at the point of care can lead to high-quality care that is safe, efficient, effective, timely, lower-cost, equitable, and universal.[3] If those characteristics are to be realized, interoperability must include establishing the integrity of the data so critical decisions can be made reliably.

Achieving interoperability must also require an understanding of the priority and persistence of data as it is shared among the various settings for healthcare: inpatient, ambulatory care, long-term care, home care, and specialty settings such as the emergency department. Dental care, pharmacies, mental health, urgent care, and other settings must also be part of the system. Interoperability requires all parties to participate—solo practitioners must be included—so that all patient data currently scattered throughout the system can be recreated in a comprehensive record at the point of care, wherever it might be.

With true interoperability, data can be interchanged or merged within an institution and among institutions, shared with the patient, and used to meet state and federal reporting requirements. Clinical decision support can be integrated seamlessly into the patient care process. Much, if not all, of clinical trial data can be derived from and integrated into patient care. Patients can receive informed care, regardless of their location.

What Is Required for True Interoperability?

Data standards are necessary for the realization of true interoperability in healthcare. Both functional and semantic interoperability require the use of uniform standards for the interchange and reuse of data by multiple parties. Additionally, semantic interoperability requires all systems to speak the same language. These standards must be adopted and implemented nationally—if uniform standards are not in place, the interoperability chain is broken. Beyond the need to have a complete record at the point of care, electronic health records must contain structured data in a structured architecture to permit its reuse. Some narrative may be permitted, but the narrative will be an enhancement of the structured data element.

The Data Element

Semantic interoperability must start with data elements, which standardize the basic components of data interchange. A reference information model, such as the Health Level 7 (HL7) Reference Information Model, provides a common framework upon which data element definitions and their relationships with other data elements can be based.[4]

The most critical attribute of the data element is a precise definition such that when a data element is reused, there is a common meaning shared by all. These definitions (and other attributes) would be validated by named experts in each clinical domain, with a broader audience involved in a feedback process. Data elements crossing multiple disciplines would be vetted by experts from each area. For example, hematologists would be responsible for identifying the data elements commonly used in their practice, but they may also provide feedback on data elements used by their relevant colleagues in the course of treatment of leukemia and other blood disorders.

The greatest barrier to semantic interoperability in today's systems is the lack of a single common vocabulary or terminology set. There are more than 200 defined, controlled terminologies, most with slightly different purposes. None of these are perfect or complete for interoperability. Some are free and others require a licensing fee. Well-known terminologies include SNOMED CT, LOINC, RxNorm, MedDRA, ICD9–CM, ICD10, CPT, and a host of others. Within these vocabularies healthcare stakeholders can communicate using the same language. But they often must be translated to other vocabularies. Mapping one to another is often attempted, but this results in the loss of information. Further, mapping never ends, it is expensive, and mapping tables are never synchronized. This patchwork creates a dizzying maze of complex technical gymnastics that could be avoided by adopting a common set of data standards.

True interoperability will be accomplished only if a single term is assigned to each data element, and the existing controlled terminologies are excellent sources for content. Additional attributes include data type and units (from a standardized set) and a value set that represents all the proper responses or values for that data element. Value sets may be constrained for a specific application without loss of interoperability. For example, the data element "administrative gender" might have the value set of "male," "female," and "unavailable."

A data element may be proposed by anyone at any time, with an automated process that takes the data element through a defining stage, a vetting stage, a testing and acceptance stage, and a trial stage, emerging as a mature data element with a single unique code that never changes. These data elements will reside in a national repository, and tools will exist to navigate and download selected elements with attributes. A number of groups are currently involved in defining data elements with attributes, including the National Cancer Institute's caBIG project, CDISC, the American College of Cardiology, the American Heart Association, and many other groups. The immediate problem is that neither the attributes nor the format of this database is standardized; similarly, there exist no standardized business rules for creating the database. These problems must be resolved.

A Consistent Template

The next structure after the data element is the template or archetype, which includes multiple data elements in a defined structure. A simple example is a compound data element such as a blood pressure measurement. In addition to the systolic pressure and the diastolic pressure, the template for blood pressure would include patient position, location of the measurement, and cuff size. Templates are registered and assigned a unique identifier. Compound data elements permit the pre-coordination of data elements.

These templates can be quite complex and define complex protocols and care plans such as a well-baby workup, a patient-admit profile, a TB screen, or a clinical-trial component. This structure could also be used for trigger-driven data transport profiles, such as when a patient is transferred from a hospital to a nursing home.

A Standard Document

The next level of standards required is document standardization, such as the HL7 Clinical Document Architecture (CDA).[5] The CDA is used for such items as radiology reports, patient summaries, discharge summaries, referrals, claims attachments, and infectious disease reports. The CDA includes a header containing such items as the document unique identifier, name, date and time stamp, sender, and receiver. The body of the document is a structure defined by an XML schema. A similar standard, the Continuity of Care Record (CCR), has been created by ASTM International.[6] The CDA and the CCR are now being blended into a single document standard called the Continuity of Care Document (CCD).[7]

The standards defined thus far provide interoperability within a single institution, as well as serving as the basis for semantic interoperability when interchanging data with other parties. The interchange of data requires communication standards such as TCP/IP,

HTTP, SOAP, and Web services protocols. XML has now become the primary syntax for all these structure standards.

A Data Interchange Standard

The most common data interchange standard for clinical data is the HL7 V2 series and the V3 series of data transport standards. The DICOM transport standard is used for imaging data; NCPDP SCRIPT standard for prescription data; ASC X12 for transaction (claims) standards; IEEE for medical device standards; and OASIS for business data. As noted, the ASTM CCR and the HL7 CDA can also be used for data interchange. One initiative, Integrating the Healthcare Environment (IHE), sponsored by the Radiological Society of North America and the Healthcare Information and Management Systems Society, is providing guidance for the end-to-end process by creating domain profiles and using existing standards.

Application Standard

The next set of required standards for true interoperability deal with application interoperability. Use cases are an excellent starting point to understand interchange of data requirements and to identify the actors, acts, and interactions. Starting with the HL7 RIM, Message Information Models define the required data interchanges, including data elements to be transferred. Data models enhance this process and provide clear understanding of interactions, players, trigger events, and information flow management.

Included within this set of standards are the HL7 EHR functional specifications that offer a base for the certification process provided by the Certification Commission for Health Information Technology (CCHIT).

Another important area enabled by interoperability standards is clinical decision support. These standards include a knowledge reference framework, knowledge representation, and the logic structures for decision rules. Other standards define clinical guidelines and disease management protocols. Examples include the Arden Syntax, Protégé, GELLO, Guideline Interchange Format (GLIF-HL7), Guidelines Elements Model (GEM-ASTM) and the HL7 Infobutton. Electronic health record content standards and architecture standards are just now beginning to be defined and include the

European standard organization CEN and the PV 13606 EHR standard.

Critical to the ability to link patient data and provider data are a series of identifiers. These identifiers are defined by the HIPAA requirements and include a facility identifier, an employer identifier, a provider identifier (the National Provider Identifier), and a personal identifier. A unique person identifier has not yet been defined and remains a significant barrier to seamlessly linking patient data.

Current solutions for a personal identifier use a number of demographic parameters, including name, date of birth, gender, race, mother's maiden name, Social Security number, and other items to establish the identity of the patient. This approach is far from perfect and must be addressed in order to achieve true interoperability. The United States is one of only a few countries that do not have a unique person identifier.

True interoperability must be built on trust, integrity, and reliability. Trust is built on effective security and privacy standards and processes. Systems must support role-based access control. In other words, certain health information may be accessed only by medical professionals, while other information may be made available to hospital administrators, insurers, and so on. Security standards include access control, authentication, authorization, repudiation, encryption, a digital signature, and access logs.

As systems progress toward true interoperability, additional standards will be required. Examples include standardized query sets to pull data for defined purposes, standardized disease management protocols, standardized core data sets derived from the master data set, standardized reporting sets, and standardized patient education modules. Additional standards are required to support the creation of data elements and the management of that process.

The Barriers

Many of the barriers to true interoperability are a result of a few specific conditions: disagreement over the term; a belief that true interoperability is impossible; a lack of understanding of where to start and/or what is required; a lack of understanding of who should do it and who should pay for it; and the absence of a well-documented business case. These barriers are significant, but they can be overcome. We must start by asking some very tough questions.

There is no clear, nationally shared vision of what we are trying to build for the nationwide health information technology infrastructure. The result can be overwhelming: What terminologies will be used? What standards will be required? What are the timelines? Who will build it? What tools will be available? Should it be created by the private sector or will the federal government provide the direction? Where will the leadership come from? Who will pay for it? If it is the private sector, how will we recover the expenses? Should patients be required to pay? What is the business case, and who profits from the purchase, installation, and use of such systems? As a provider, what if I choose a system that does not become the national choice? Should I wait until the type I want is implemented? I do not have control over the vendors—must I be required to accept what is offered?

Despite these unanswered questions, there are seeds that can grow. Most medium to large healthcare facilities have some sort of computerized information system. Whether these systems are really EHR systems is debatable, as there is no common definition of what constitutes an EHR. Most academic medical systems have more than one health information technology system installed, and these systems are typically a mixture of commercial systems, home-grown systems, and joint developments.

Departments within a facility or organization generally do not wish to change systems, and the interoperable solution will require each system to meet the standards discussed above. The first step to national interoperability is for each healthcare facility to adopt and implement the required standards for interoperability and require their systems to comply—whether homegrown or commercial. An initial step would be the adoption of standardized data elements with a standardized terminology and value sets and the creation of a merged patient-centric EHR for the sharing of patient data within the institution. From that position, data can then be exchanged with a Regional Health Information Organization (RHIO) or for other business purposes.

The creation of a Nationwide Health Information Network (NHIN) and the opportunity to share data seamlessly with other sites requires all participants to meet the interoperability requirements. How is that effort synchronized? RHIOs are the current answers to beginning components of the NHIN, and they are mostly forced to deal with data as it currently exists and is available to them. In most cases, that data is largely unstructured, uses a combination of terminologies of mostly local vocabularies, and is undefined. The data cannot be merged and is available only in independent display mode. Although there is some value to this approach, the achievements possible with true interoperability cannot be realized. Synchroniza-tion of the change to interoperability must be led from a national level and implemented on a local level.

Healthcare facilities are neither financially nor operationally prepared to make the changes necessary for achieving true interoperability. Long-range plans and budgets do not accommodate the resources necessary to support this change.

What is the timeline for implementing interoperable systems? Do we set a target date in the future and move toward it at an independent pace? Are the goals set two years in the future, five years, ten years, or even twenty years? That is up for discussion, as wise people can disagree on how aggressively to move. Whatever the timeline, it is important to keep in mind how quckly new technology becomes available. Examples include advancements in processing speed, storage size, cost, growth of the Internet, handheld devices, wireless, sensors, nanotechnologies, and so on. Moore's Law is indeed alive and well. Specific timelines must be short and achievable, and efforts must be coordinated. Endpoints must be clearly set, or we will simply be solving a different problem with different tools.

For the most part, with current models, the persons paying for and supporting the movement to an interoperable HIT system do not receive the financial benefits from such changes. Patients and payers will benefit, but a well-designed system should provide some benefit to the facility installing the system, be it a solo practitioner or complex institution.

Issues of privacy and security of data represent major barriers. These issues are important not only for patients, but also for providers, and even for institutions that worry about the loss of a marketing edge if details of their operation are known in real time. There is a fear of big government or big business peeking at our clinical data and taking advantage of that knowledge. Patients are afraid of loss of employment or insurability. Others are concerned with sensitive private data. The pros and cons of an NHIN must be determined and a convincing argument made to the public. Americans must buy in to the idea that their quality of life will be much better and satisfaction with the healthcare system will be higher through the use of interoperable HIT systems.

Stakeholders and the Use of Interoperable Data

Historically, the use of IT in healthcare has been to support the administrative and reimbursement processes. Clinical systems were at first departmental systems supporting clinical laboratory, radiology, pharmacy, materials management, and service functions such as admissions, discharges, and transfers. Clinical systems, such as the electronic health record, are still in a minority and are frequently independent of the administrative and service system. Inroads have been made through the use of Computerized Physician Order Entry (CPOE) systems and electronic prescribing systems. That world must change.

The reuse of data permits the integration of the interests of all stakeholders in the healthcare process. That list includes the patient; providers of care; administrators; payers; regulators; auditors; local, state, and federal governments; the military; educators; researchers; pharmaceutical companies; technology vendors; consultants; employers; law enforcement; emergency responders; and many others. All these stakeholders should participate in defining the interoperability requirements and be willing to integrate their needs into the common system by sharing and reusing data.

The use of patient care data for clinical research is workable and would save considerable expense in the duplicate collection of data. Candidates for clinical trials would be identified by the computer from semantic interoperable data, permission would be obtained from the patient, and the data would be integrated into the research data base without requiring human resources. The size of clinical trials could expand by orders of magnitude. Those researching cures for rare diseases would encounter less trouble in identifying participants in those trials. All individuals taking a drug could participate in the drug study, given patient consent. Using common data elements with precise definitions would enable this process.

The reimbursement process is one of the most inefficient processes in the healthcare system and uses an unbelievable amount of human resources. If healthcare plans were precisely identified (a HIPAA requirement not yet achieved) and defined in a standard that supported semantic and functional interoperability, those plans could be imbedded in EHR systems, and reimbursement could be accomplished in close to real time (accommodating late charges). Approvals for tests and treatment would be made in real time. If a test was not approved, an alternative could be suggested as part of the real-time, point-of-care process. The savings generated by such an integrated reimbursement system should more than pay for such a system, and patient satisfaction should be high.

Increasingly, patients must play a responsible role in their healthcare. Personal health records (PHRs) are a way to engage consumers. Access to their own healthcare data can alert patients about actions they need to take to treat their conditions, such as a Hemoglobin A1c test every six months, follow-up tests for statins, and advice relating to modification of behavior. These are only a few benefits of PHRs.

Natural disasters such as hurricanes and earthquakes have provided excellent business cases for true interoperability, EHRs, and the NHIN. In the case of Hurricane Katrina and its aftermath, interoperable regional patient summary records could have been used to identify who needed to be evacuated—pregnant women close to their due dates, patients on dialysis, patients on respirators, disabled patients, and patients without means of transportation to evacuate, to name just a few.

As the evacuation of the Gulf Coast progressed and patients went to all parts of the country and received care, that healthcare, for the most part, was delivered blindly and without triage because caregivers had virtually no access to information. Access to an EHR would have saved many lives. The Veterans Administration EHR system, VistA, was in use in the New Orleans area. Tapes containing patient data were carried to other sites and made available over the Internet to the facility where the veteran next received care. Research is underway to provide the details of the numbers and what was accomplished by making this data available at the new points of care.

A similar opportunity exists for detection of a bio-attack. Monitoring symptoms and activity regionally as well as nationally will be the first step in detecting such an attack. Health information technology has already demonstrated its power in detecting and controlling such diseases as SARS, Avian flu, and AIDS.

The broad community of stakeholders must work together toward the effective and timely employment of interoperable systems. We need approaches to bring this community together—not just the leadership, but also the workers with the expertise to create products.

What Needs to Happen to Get There?

A number of countries have committed to building national health information networks based on concepts discussed in this chapter, including the goal of empowering citizens with personal health records. Leaders include the United Kingdom, Canada, Australia, New Zealand, Denmark, and the United States. The healthcare systems of these countries differ greatly, as do the starting points and implementation strategies. Time will tell which approaches work and which do not.

The U.S. may have the most difficult task in creating a truly interoperable NHIN. It is constrained by such issues as a large, established base of different systems; lack of control of stakeholders; inability to establish common priorities; requirement of an irrefutable business case; lack of a national vision; public/private differences in control, funding, and responsibilities; mismatch in expenditures and benefits; and other factors.

But policymakers and private-sector leaders have taken some steps that will help define the path to success. We are fortunate that President George W. Bush and his administration have made the adoption of health information technology a top priority. From the creation of the Office of the National Coordinator for Health Information Technology to Health and Human Services Secretary Mike Leavitt's formation of the American Health Information Community, the federal government has begun to provide timely and much-needed leadership in creating the NHIN.

Additionally, the creation of the Certification Commission for Health Information Technology to certify EHR products is an essential next step, and that process must be expanded to require the use of standards necessary for end-to-end interoperability. The Health Information Technology Standards Panel is responsible for harmonizing the work of existing Standards Developer Organizations and identifying the required standards, noting which exist and which are required. While these activities are important, that effort alone will not lead us to true interoperability.

Solving the interoperability dilemma will require a process similar to building the interstate highway system in the U.S. The framework for the interstate system and the specification standards were defined nationally. A roadmap was developed that provided a vision for the national network. Funding was allocated by the federal government and the states. Related projects were even funded at local levels. The plan was then executed at the state level, where it was passed to regional and local levels for execution. By utilizing national standards, the interstate highways system provides a reasonably consistent national network of compatible highways.

So what must be done in healthcare? Some tough problems that have been around for many years must be solved.

First, we need a unique, national identifier for every person in America. A public education campaign will most certainly be needed, specifically focusing on explaining the need and value of linking records through a unique individual identifier.

Second, all stakeholders must agree upon a common terminology.

Third, all stakeholders, including payers, must use these standardized data elements with a single terminology. The use of multiple terminologies is an enormous obstacle to the exchange of patient data, and true interoperability requires the rules to be the same and the use of interoperability standards to be the same.

Fourth, the leadership of healthcare institutions must be totally committed to modernizing healthcare through information technology, from large group practices to hospital systems to health plans.

Fifth, we need a national leader who can clearly articulate what can be done and what is to be done at a national level. We need a leader who can make the case that health information technology is a top priority. This should be a collaborative process between the public and private sectors, but all must embrace a common strategy of success.

Sixth, the vendor community must be brought into the process to help educate all stakeholders about when and how the use of the standards will be achieved.

Seventh, we need to develop a sustainable funding model. The value and savings that can be demonstrated through interoperability is more than enough to pay for the NHIN.

Lastly, we need a feasible timeline with specific plans for who performs what and when.

We can do this. We can succeed. Let's get moving.

—⁂—

W. Edward Hammond, Ph.D., is Professor Emeritus, Department of Community and Family Medicine, Professor Emeritus, Department of Biomedical Engineering, Duke University, and Adjunct Professor in the Fuqua School of Business at Duke University. He is a past President of the American Medical Informatics Association (AMIA). He has twice served as the Chair of Health Level 7 and is current Chair-elect. He is Vice Chair of the HL7 Technical Steering Committee and chair of the Advisory Committee. He was Chair of the Data Standards Working Group of the Connecting for Health Public-Private Consortium. Dr. Hammond was a member of the Institute of Medicine Committee on Patient Safety Data Standards. He served as President of the American College of Medical Informatics and as Chair of the Computer-based Patient Record Institute. He served as the Convenor of ISO Technical Committee 215, Working Group 2 for six years and is currently ISO TC 215's Ambassador to

Developing Countries. He is a founding fellow of ACMI and AIMBE. He was a member of the National Library of Medicine Long Range Planning Committee (2006) and a member of the Healthcare Information Technology Advisory Panel of the Joint Commission on Accreditation of Healthcare Organizations (2006). He is an advisor to the American Hospital Association Information Technology Standards Initiative Strategy Committee. Dr. Hammond was awarded the Paul Ellwood Lifetime Achievement Award in 2003 and the ACMI Morris F. Collen Award of Excellence in November 2003.

—◊—

[1] Institute of Electrical and Electronics Engineers, *IEEE Standard Computer Dictionary: A Compilation of IEEE Standard Computer Glossaries* (New York: IEEE, 1991).

[2] The National Alliance for Health Information Technology, "What Is Interoperability?" 2006. Available at http://www.nahit.org/cms/index.php?option=com_content&task=view&id=186&Itemid=195 (accessed April 2, 2007).

[3] Institute of Medicine, *Crossing the Quality Chasm: A New Health System for the 21st Century* (Washington, D.C.: National Academy Press, 2001).

[4] Health Level Seven, Inc., "HL7 Reference Information Model." Available at http://www.hl7.org/Library/data-model/RIM/modelpage_mem.htm (accessed April 6, 2007).

[5] Health Level Seven, Inc., "HL7 Clinical Document Architecture, Release 2.0," Available at http://www.hl7.org (accessed March 23, 2007).

[6] ASTM International, ASTM E 2369, "Standard Specification for Continuity of Care Record (CCR)," 2005. Referenced ASTM standards available at www.astm.org.

[7] Health Level Seven, Inc., "HL7 Continuity of Care Document." Available at http://www.hl7.org (accessed March 23, 2007).

CHAPTER 4

A Personal Health Record for Every American: Connecting Consumers to Connect Healthcare

Edward Fotsch, M.D.

—⋘—

Editor's Introduction

Healthcare consumerism is here to stay. The introduction and growing popularity of high-deductible health plans coupled with Health Savings Accounts and the growing need to influence consumer health behavior has formally ushered in this new era. Lifting the veil of healthcare pricing and provider performance has taken consumer-driven healthcare to another level. It will reach even greater heights when consumers have the appropriate tools and proper incentives to manage their health and healthcare. Personal health records are the key to this. So far, the adoption of these tools has been slow, but it is not for lack of sophistication. Innovators like HealthTrio and Medem are introducing new features to their personal health record systems every day. The problem rests with the healthcare system at large, which until recently has functionally ignored consumers and badly misaligned consumer incentives. With new financing models, chronic care management, and proper incentives, personal health records will be the most powerful and effective way for Americans to become engaged. This will increase consumer demand for these services, undoubtedly transforming health and healthcare.

—⋘—

It is true, as the title of this book suggests: paper kills.

Clipboards are paper's accomplice. The unfortunate reality of today's healthcare system is that a great deal of care is based on patient histories supplied by the patient or by family members, derived from notes handwritten on a clipboard in a waiting room. Follow-up care is based primarily on paper records and intermittent phone calls between provider visits, with little consistent patient support in between. Consumers can search health topics online, but they cannot access their own records or their providers. There ought to be a better way, and there is.

Health information technology that replaces paper and makes information and communication securely available to patients and providers does in fact save lives. Consumer engagement in information technology can create the market drivers to eliminate paper in healthcare, as it has in many other industries, from banking to travel to retail shopping.

Personal health records (PHRs) are the primary tools that connect consumers directly to their own health information and to their chosen healthcare providers. If we are to truly transform health and healthcare, we must harness consumer demand and aggressively engage consumers and providers with health information technology—and PHRs are the surest way to succeed.

What Is a Personal Health Record?

Until recently, the extent of information exchange between patients and providers was based largely upon the information that a patient could recall and write out on a form while waiting for an office appointment or hospital admission. This included basic patient information such as current medications, conditions, allergies, demographic information, insurance, and whatever else the patient or family member can remember to tell a provider. Most patients have little access to professional medical records when they register for care with a provider. Patients may have received a copy of their medical record from a single physician or hospital, but until recently there was no clear mechanism for convenient storage, access, and exchange of health information in one central location that could build over time. Patients had no ability to create a longitudinal health record spanning years, geography, and multiple care providers. Nor could they access this record anytime, anywhere.

Just as technology has changed the landscape of so many industries, it is now slowly creeping into healthcare. Consumers now have tools at their fingertips that allow them to own a comprehensive and portable version of their health records. These personal health records allow consumers to keep a thorough and lifelong record of their healthcare. When executed from a standards-based system that complies with state and federal privacy laws, PHRs provide a secure and confidential tool for patients to manage their health information in partnership with their chosen providers. This transition has magnified the potential power of a PHR from a static collection of paper-based information to an interactive, online communication platform that allows patients to be more efficiently involved in their own care.

In 2003, the Markle Foundation's Connecting for Health initiative, a collaborative working group of government agencies and industry leaders with a goal of advancing technology information systems in healthcare, published what has become the basis for an industry definition of a PHR: "an Internet-based set of tools that allows people to access and coordinate their lifelong health information and make appropriate parts of it available to those who need it."[1] In August of that same year, Harris Interactive confirmed in a national survey that there is overwhelming interest in PHR services when delivered in the context of the patient-physician relationship, including online communication and data-sharing.[2]

A more recent survey from Accenture has shown that consumers not only value PHR functionality, but they will choose healthcare providers based upon those who offer these services, and they indicate that they are willing to pay for these services.[3] Health Level Seven (HL7), a standards-developing organization made up of experts in the exchange of electronic healthcare information, is now finalizing a more detailed set of requirements for PHRs based largely on the Markle definition.

Basic functionality of PHRs includes:

- The ability to store all relevant healthcare information in one central online location that allows 24/7 access from anywhere with Internet connectivity (especially helpful in a medical emergency)
- The ability to grant others (physicians, family members, caregivers) access to this record (or portions of it), providing greater accuracy when transferring health information, particularly among multiple providers
- The portability of health information when a patient travels, changes jobs, changes providers, or moves to a new place
- The ability to allow information exchange and updates from treating physicians, pharmacies, health plans, or other third-party sources

- The option to use the personal health record as a communications platform. Some personal health records offer secure online messaging between patient and physician, automated education tailored to specific conditions or treatments, reminder messaging, online appointment scheduling, prescription refill requests, and access to risk-assessment and wellness tools.

None of this can happen on paper. No clipboard can give consumers access to a comprehensive health record in real time. No paper file can allow patients to communicate with their physicians in an effective way. No paper-based record sitting in a file cabinet can save a life in an emergency. PHRs can do this and much more. They help patients manage their health by giving them control over their own health information,[4] providing supportive disease management and health promotion education, and connecting them to their physicians. In the end, personal health records represent the surest way to engage consumers to improve their health, streamline the administration of care, and improve the overall efficiency and quality of care.

Why PHRs? Why Now?

Several forces are driving the rise in PHRs and their use. Healthcare costs continue to climb (currently at 16 percent of the GDP, with annual increase projected at 7.7 percent through 2010[5]), and as the largest healthcare payer, the federal government is aligned with commercial payers in looking for health IT innovations to improve care and reduce cost. Mounting evidence suggests PHRs positively affect both quality of care and cost. Government leaders, including President George W. Bush, Secretary of Health and Human Services Mike Leavitt, and leaders of the Centers for Medicare and Medicaid Services (CMS) have identified personal health records as a priority in their push to improve and advance the U.S. healthcare system. Other payers, such as health plans and employers, are also looking to health IT for ways to cut costs by improving efficiency, supporting treatment adherence, and promoting wellness and prevention. Many payers, including CMS, are beginning to establish financial incentives for providers to use such technologies.

In addition, the momentum of consumer-driven healthcare initiatives, particularly high-deductible health plans with Health Savings Accounts, has created a marketplace where people are "shopping" for care and consumers are increasingly empowered. PHRs can be a powerful tool for consumers—some have tools that allow people to compare prices among providers, while others have quality indicators on provider performance. More advanced PHR technologies have made them easier to use and available at little or no cost to the patient.

PHRs also offer a cost-effective way to help reduce medical errors by helping ensure patients' medical information is complete. With the proliferation of widely publicized statistics on medical errors in recent years, as well as services now offering patients "report cards" on hospitals and physicians, patient safety initiatives are front-and-center for both patients and providers. The Institute of Medicine's groundbreaking report on medical errors, *To Err Is Human,* raised national awareness that improving health systems can reduce patient deaths.[6] PHRs can play an important role by helping patients become managers of their own health, thereby offering physicians more accurate personal health information about their patients at the point of care. PHRs also can be used as part of an automated system to alert physicians of drug interactions or contraindications—thereby reducing the risk of injury.

PHRs have the potential to benefit healthcare across the industry, including patients, physicians, payers, government, and the public health at large. The marriage of market necessity and clinical relevance has positioned PHRs at the crossroads of transforming health.

Who Uses PHRs?

Results of a 2004 nationwide survey by Harris Interactive found that 42 percent of people in this country keep some form of personal medical record. Of those who do not have a personal medical record, the overwhelming majority (84 percent) think keeping one is a good idea. And while only 13 percent of those who already have a personal health record keep it electronically, 40 percent of those who do not thought it was "at least somewhat likely" that they would create one in an electronic format.[7]

The Harris Interactive poll also found:

- Women (45 percent) are more likely than men (38 percent) to keep personal or family medical records.
- Older people are more likely than younger people to keep personal or family medical records. Fully 58 percent of people over 65 do so.

Other national surveys have reported that the majority of the population (even those not aware of PHRs) is interested in the benefits PHRs provide. In concert with the Markle Foundation, the Foundation for Accountability (FACCT) conducted a national survey to gain insight into public perception and adoption of PHRs. The FACCT survey found "large majorities of patients and consumers indicate that they would use key PHR services as they are needed—when filling a prescription, sharing information with new doctors, understanding how to care for their own illnesses, or helping a frail parent."[8] (Additional survey results in box to the right.)

Of the 1,246 online households surveyed, FACCT found the greatest interest in PHRs comes from patients who are chronically ill, those frequently receiving healthcare, or people caring for elderly parents. Similarly, iHealthRecord.org estimates more than 30 percent of the first 100,000+ individuals who had built a PHR on their network are caregivers of a child, a chronically ill patient, or an elderly parent.

Markle Foundation Survey Results	
Over 70 percent of respondents would use one or more features of the PHR to:	
• E-mail my doctor	75%
• Track immunizations	69%
• Note mistakes in my record	69%
• Transfer information to new doctors	65%
• Get and track my test results	63%

The chronically ill, frequent users of healthcare, and people caring for elderly parents report the highest and most urgent interest in PHRs. Almost two-thirds (65 percent) of people whith chronic illness say they would use at least one of the PHR features today.

Chronically ill or elderly patients likely have multiple health providers and need greater coordination within their healthcare "community." PHR systems can offer a central location for information exchange among caregivers, physicians, and other healthcare providers, helping to ensure that everyone knows of pertinent lab results, prescriptions, treatment regimens, and/or other information necessary for coordinating high-quality and cost-efficient care.

For healthy patients, PHRs offer an opportunity for improved care due to more accurate and effective information transfer and sharing. The greatest appeal, however, may prove to be the conveniences built into PHR systems, such as secure messaging with physicians, online appointment scheduling, and Web-enabled prescription refills. The Institute for the Future reported 70 percent of adults ages 25 to 34 want online access to their health information.[9]

Patient adoption of PHRs is rising, and according to the National Committee on Vital and Health Statistics, consumers and patients who use PHR systems express strong support for them.[10] The potential benefits of PHRs extend to all patients. If the majority of patients were aware of the benefits and convenience of PHRs, they would demand these services and create more market-based pressure for physicians to offer the service. If the majority of patients used PHRs, the positive impact on the healthcare system would be significant. Patients would be encouraged to be active participants in their care, efficient information exchange across healthcare delivery systems would cut costs, and access to real-time information would result in fewer medical errors.

Some question the issue of online access among the poor and underprivileged portions of the population. Interesting new developments are making this less of an issue. One case in point is the use of PHRs to provide a continuum-of-care record for migrant workers—a highly mobile, poor, and often non-English-speaking population. Clinics are using PHR technologies to create a basic health record for their patients, capturing information regarding demographics, medications, conditions, etc., which can be updated by any clinic the worker visits, anywhere in the country. And for services that offer the capability, the clinic can print a wallet card and instruct the recipient on its at other clinics, in emergencies, and so on.

Hospitals and health systems in low-income areas are beginning to provide a similar service for their patients. In addition, senior citizens' organizations, libraries, and other public offices can and are facilitating access to online services for visitors not able to provide it for themselves. Because of the potential benefit to this population of patients, ways to bridge any access gap must continue to be explored.

Patient Benefits of PHRs

Of every stakeholder in healthcare, patients will gain the most from using PHRs, as these technologies can have profound results for their health. PHRs offer individuals the opportunity to be proactive in their care, improve communication and coordination with their healthcare team, receive better disease and condition management (especially in cases of multiple co-morbidities), benefit from patient safety initiatives, experience improved emergency treatment outcomes, participate in preventive care and wellness promotion, and experience greater convenience and consumer satisfaction.

PHRs are of particular value to non-professional caregivers, often working women who are juggling the healthcare needs of children, spouses, aging parents, and themselves. A national survey published in the *Wall Street Journal* noted that more than 50 percent of women ages 45 to 50 were simultaneously caring for both a child and a parent. Helping organize the healthcare information of multiple family members can mean huge gains for these individuals in terms of efficiency, accuracy of medical information, and peace of mind.

As people are experiencing greater mobility (both traveling and relocating), living longer, and taking more medications then ever before, there is a need to bridge the fragmentation of healthcare with both a continuum of care as well as a coordination of care among providers. The number one reason given by patients to have a PHR

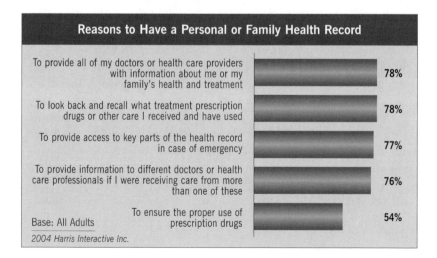

Reasons to Have a Personal or Family Health Record

To provide all of my doctors or health care providers with information about me or my family's health and treatment	78%
To look back and recall what treatment prescription drugs or other care I received and have used	78%
To provide access to key parts of the health record in case of emergency	77%
To provide information to different doctors or health care professionals if I were receiving care from more than one of these	76%
To ensure the proper use of prescription drugs	54%

Base: All Adults

2004 Harris Interactive Inc.

is "to provide all of my doctors or healthcare providers with information about me or my family's health and treatment."[11] The portability of PHRs offers patients a way to bridge the information gap created by isolated and episodic medical care.

Disease Management and Health Promotion

Communication platforms built into PHRs can automate educational messaging specific to a patient regarding prevention, wellness, early detection, and disease/condition management. PHR systems can improve both medication adherence and behavioral change by:

- *Providing Clear Instructions:* Just because patients tell their doctors they understand treatment instructions does not always mean they will remember those instructions later on. A 2003 study published by the Royal Society of Medicine reported that up to 80 percent of the information provided from physician to patient is forgotten by the time the patient leaves the doctor's office, and that of the information patients do retain, almost 50 percent is remembered incorrectly.[12] A PHR can store instructions, helping to avoid the confusion that sometimes leads to serious consequences. An online record and automated reminders of treatment instructions cannot be lost or misplaced, as can a piece of paper. Although simple, this asset to care management can have substantial results.

- *Providing Disease Management Education Messages and Resources:* Education resources contained within PHRs further engage patients by facilitating outreach from the provider to the patient, enabling access to additional information about their conditions. In a Connecticut-based clinical trial, physicians used Medem's PHR, called iHealthRecord, to provide disease management services to patients taking statins and anti-depressants, including secure, HIPAA-complaint e-mail reminders to encourage compliance with drug and therapy regimens. One hundred study participants were surveyed regarding their experiences receiving medication. After six months of use, survey results showed:

  – 66 percent of patients believed that the adherence messages they received help them better understand their

medication and better manage their condition
  – 95 percent of patients believed that the adherence service
    "is an important part of helping busy doctors provide extra
    care and information to patients"
  – 85 percent of patients wished to continue receiving adher-
    ence messages from their physicians

Additionally, a review of claims data showed a more than 40 percent reduction in medication drop-off (6 percent for the study group
versus 10.5 percent for the control group).[13] Thus, PHRs can be an
important tool to increase compliance and improve patient health.

Increased Patient Safety

PHRs can facilitate patient awareness of issues with a drug or medical device. For example, if the FDA issues a recall or patient advisory
regarding a medication, a warning or alert-type announcement can
be transmitted to patients in real time. In some cases, this can be
life-saving. Such warnings can be a powerful way to help reduce the
estimated 7,000 people who die each year from preventable medication errors.[14]

Emergency Care

In an emergency, having the ability to access a patient's medical
information at the point of care can be life-saving. Twenty-five percent of Americans mistakenly think that emergency rooms automatically have access to their health information.[15] The implications of
PHR access in critical care situations is especially applicable with elderly patients, who may be geographically far from family members or
unable to provide accurate and detailed health information about
themselves. Whether the patient is young or old, if a physician in an
emergency situation can access a person's updated and accurate
basic medical history through a PHR, there are untold benefits to
the quality of care the patient receives.

Provider Benefits of PHRs

In addition to financial benefits to their practices, PHRs offer many
of the same benefits to physicians as they do to patients: better
patient care because of a more complete, efficient, and accurate

exchange of information; a reduction in medical errors; and improved patient treatment adherence and outcomes. The vertical view of a patient's health history can be of further help to physicians by tracking the status of a patient's condition as well as treatment progress or adverse events. It also enables a more complete medical history from which providers can locate trends or other issues that may need attention.

PHRs can show not only whether a medication was prescribed, but also whether it was filled. The PHR is a "window" into the continuum of a patient's health—a more complete picture that can help physicians provide better care and can allow patients the resources to engage in managing their own care. PHRs can also:

- Help physicians with requirements of pay-for-performance programs, including the new NCQA member services categories, Bridges to Excellence, and financial incentives tied to PHRs likely to be instituted by programs within the federal department of Health and Human Services, particularly the Centers for Medicare and Medicaid Services (CMS)
- Lead to a reduction in medical liability risk because of improved documentation of patient notes and better communication.
  (Professional liability carriers have actively endorsed the use of appropriate PHR services)
- Provide physicians with a market advantage due to improved patient satisfaction and convenience, as well as patient demand for new technologies in their physician's office
- Provide direct revenue to physicians who offer electronic consults and communication to their patients

Improved Doctor-Patient Relationship

Not surprisingly, in a time when the many administrative and other financial burdens of managed care have constrained physicians' time, patients are seeking additional ways to connect with their physicians. Approximately 90 percent of adults with Internet access would like to be able to communicate with their doctors online.[16] PHRs provide a simple, direct way to have these communications. The physician can communicate without feeling rushed, and the patient can read—and store—the physician's message for reference. This allows patients to be more involved in and take greater responsibility for their own healthcare.

The effect of patient access to a Web-based online medical record with communication capacities was analyzed in a randomized trial of patients suffering from congestive heart failure. The study's authors concluded that such access to online personal health information and online exchanges between patients and physicians resulted in better satisfaction with doctor-patient communication, improved adherence, and no adverse affects.[17]

Better Patient Outcomes and Increased Patient Engagement

Behavior interventions and medication adherence launched from PHR systems can lead to better patient outcomes. Survey data and the experience of numerous commercial disease management firms confirm the CMS assertion that automated patient engagement using PHRs and similar online tools does have a positive impact on patient behavior and understanding.[18]

- *Medication Adherence:* Poor medication adherence is among the frequently cited reasons for poor disease management. A review of scientific literature by the World Health Organization estimated that patients with chronic conditions take their medications as prescribed only 50 percent of the time.[19] As described in the "Patient Benefits" section above, clear instructions on how to take medications, ongoing educational messages on why medication is needed, and prescription refill reminders can help motivate patients to manage their heath. All of this can happen through a well-designed PHR.

- *Behavioral Intervention Adherence:* With nearly one-quarter of all adults in the U.S. classified as obese and at risk for serious associated conditions,[20] and a substantial number smoking or struggling with substance abuse, facilitating behavioral interventions and support to help patients adhere to lifestyle changes has become an important part of primary care and preventive medicine. Ongoing Web-based messages on how to incorporate lifestyle changes, interactive tools (online body mass index calculators, portion calculators, exercise logs, etc.), and regular messages of encouragement from their physicians or healthcare providers can help coach patients to better health while simultaneously providing a record for patients and physicians to review.

Although much of the relationship between behavioral changes and online intervention is presumptive, a growing number of studies have documented a positive correlation between Internet-based provider communications and improved adherence to recommended lifestyle changes. One such study documented an improvement in annual mammography rates among women who received automated mammogram reminders from their providers[21] while a similar study looked at e-mail counseling as a weight loss intervention for adults at risk for type-2 diabetes. The result: the addition of e-mail counseling to a basic weight loss program resulted in significantly greater weight loss.[22]

Improved Documentation, Increased Quality of Care, and the Potential for Decreased Liability

There are unquestioned benefits when a patient and physician communicate openly and honestly after a diagnosis or course of treatment has been made. For physicians, having a record of the process not only helps track a patient's progress, but in the event of an allegation of negligence, the documentation can help clarify what was said and done and when. For patients, having physicians' instructions in a PHR can help avoid situations where the patient forgets and may feel embarrassed by having to ask again.

The PHR allows the physician and patient to be on the same page, avoiding confusion and increasing the likelihood of patient compliance. Moreover, the PHR contains the complete history of all the patient's physicians. As medical conditions become more complex and patients are seen by a greater number of specialists and allied health professionals, the PHR not only helps the patient keep track of who said what, but can help ensure each physician knows what treatments the patient has undergone and what medications have been prescribed. Having all the information on a PHR standardizes it in a manner that allows a physician to quickly get a complete picture of the patient's previous and ongoing care—arguably providing a mutually beneficial patient-physician encounter for future care.

Reduced Risk of Medical Errors

Drug database alerts to medication interactions and contraindications, as well as documentation of past adverse events and more accurate health histories, can help reduce errors.

There are new national patient safety goals issued by the Joint Commission of Accreditation of Healthcare Organizations regarding medications across the continuum of care. Through the use of PHRs to store and share medication information, these requirements can be met effectively and efficiently.

> ### Hospitals' National Patient Safety Goals 2005
>
> **Goal: Accurately and completely reconcile medications across the continuum of care.**
>
> • During 2005, for full implementation by January 2006, develop a process for obtaining and documenting a complete list of the patient's current medications upon the patient's admission to the organization and with the involvement of the patient. This process includes a comparison of the medications the organization provides to those on the list.
>
> • A complete list of the patient's medications is communicated to the next provider of service when it refers or transfers a patient to another setting, service, practitioner, or level of care within or outside the organization.

Public Health Benefits

PHR communication platforms can help facilitate information exchange from private practice to public health agencies. If patients choose to participate, aggregate information from PHRs could help public health officials track disease patterns, treatment outcomes, vaccination protection rates, and adverse reactions to medications and vaccinations. The majority of patients (62 percent) surveyed by the Markle Connecting for Health Working Group said they would release depersonalized medical information in order to improve healthcare quality.[23]

Implications for Natural Disaster Response

Natural disasters make the vulnerability of paper record-keeping all too clear. Displacement can cause interruptions in medical care, and obstacles to retrieving or accessing medical records may be insurmountable. Hundreds of thousands of Americans had such an experience during Hurricane Katrina, and their plight highlighted the need for *transportable* personal health records. As evacuees sought medical attention in communities across the U.S., many lacked access to even their most basic health information. Perhaps not surprisingly, Louisiana State University has been a leader in the delivery of fully transportable PHRs for their patients. Both their physicians and their patients know all too well the importance of being able to access critical patient information in an emergency.

In cases of displacement, a PHR can help patients and providers identify what medications and dosing schedules are required and enable healthcare professionals to access medical history and current treatment regimens from a patient's temporary place of residence. Health IT played a role in helping to alleviate some of the medical crises created by Katrina. Medical volunteers offered displaced hurricane victims on-the-spot creation of PHRs from organizations like Medem and the use of the iHealthRecord. Other efforts, like the creation of KatrinaHealth.org, a collaborative effort of medical societies, pharmacies, and the city of New Orleans, continue to provide people affected by the hurricane a way to allow their physicians and pharmacists access to their pre-Katrina electronic prescription records.

Today's Solution: Integrated PHR Systems with Provider Connectivity

PHRs that offer the full spectrum of benefits for patients, physicians, payers, and other healthcare professionals are referred to as *integrated* PHR systems. A truly integrated system is Web-based to ensure portability, compiles patient data from all these sources, securely exchanges information from several distinct entities, and offers communications options such as scheduling, online consultations, and prescription refills.

National rollout of dozens of PHR services confirm that the highest and best use of a PHR is to offer patients an integrated record and a simple yet comprehensive way to connect with their physicians. While stand-alone health plan member portal PHRs have consistently shown consumer uptake at or less than 1 percent, provider-based PHRs, such as the iHealthRecord, report a greater than 50 percent consumer uptake of PHR registration and consumer use. And under-utilized payer-only PHRs have given health plans the opportunity to examine the reason for poor consumer uptake. The

Key Potential Benefits of PHRs and PHR Systems	
ROLES	**BENEFITS**
Consumers, Patients and Their Caregivers	Support wellness activities Improve understanding of health issues Increase sense of control over health Increase control over access to personal health information Support timely, appropriate preventive services Support healthcare decisions and responsibility for care Strengthen communication with providers Verify accuracy of information in provider records Support home monitoring for chronic diseases Support understanding and appropriate use of medications Support continuity of care across time and providers Manage insurance benefits and claims Avoid duplicate tests Reduce adverse drug interactions and allergic reactions Reduce hassle through online appointment scheduling and prescription refills Increase access to providers via e-visits
Healthcare Providers	Improve access to data from other providers and the patients themselves Increase knowledge of potential drug interactions and allergies Avoid duplicate tests Improve medication compliance Provide information to patients for both healthcare and patient services purposes Provide patients with convenient access to specific information or services (e.g., lab results, Rx refills, e-visits) Improve documentation of communication with patients
Payers	Improve customer service (transactions and information) Promote portability of patient information across plan Support wellness and preventive care Provide information and education to beneficiaries
Employers	Support wellness and preventive care Provide convenient service Improve workplace productivity Promote empowered healthcare consumers Use aggregate data to manage employee health
Societal / Population Health Benefits	Strengthen health promotion and disease prevention Improve the health of populations Expand health education opportunities

overwhelming message from consumers is that provider engagement is required to engender patient value and use. This is because, not surprisingly:

- Patients trust and prefer information and tools that come from their own physicians.
- The majority of consumers are concerned about misuse of their healthcare information by employers.[24]
- The need for consumers to fill out clipboard paperwork in order to see a healthcare provider represents both an inconvenience for patients and a shortfall in the collection of information for providers. Physicians can eliminate the clipboard and improve collection of data and overall patient care through use of the PHR as a registration tool. This is a primary objective of HHS and Secretary Leavitt.

PHRs as the Rosetta Stone of Health Information Technology

Healthcare providers who replace clipboards with online PHRs can rapidly enroll the majority of those most ill into online services that can deliver integrated care management and patient education services; the result is that providers are able to quickly deliver care to consumers. And well-designed PHR services offer provider practices multiple benefits at a low cost. Rewards include increased office efficiency, lowered liability and improved documentation, and increased market share and direct revenue.

For these reasons, medical societies, patient advocacy groups, and liability carriers are actively promoting the use of PHR services by healthcare providers. And HHS/CMS should join them. Motivated providers and patients will prioritize and utilize basic HIT services that are simple, powerful, and strategic, thereby increasing the overall market demand not just for PHRs, but for all the systems that will help keep PHRs accurate and make healthcare more consumer-friendly and convenient. Harnessing consumer demand for healthcare IT will bring to life President Bush's vision of an electronic personal health record for every American.

Implementation of online PHRs will catalyze a series of steps driven by existing market forces and engaged consumers that will accelerate the national adoption of health IT and sustain its growth by making healthcare information consumer- and market-relevant.

PHRs offer the healthcare industry the opportunity to make basic patient information available across the continuum of care while engaging consumers directly in health information technology. If consumers shop for healthcare providers with an eye toward convenience, online communication, and an end of paperwork, health information technology will rapidly flourish. And "deaths from paper" will become a relic of the old 20th century health system.

—⁂—

Edward Fotsch, M.D., is chief executive officer of Medem Inc., the corporation founded in 1999 by the nation's medical societies and the AMA to deliver secure online physician-patient communications. Dr. Fotsch has more than ten years of experience in the practice of medicine and was the founding chairman of a Northern California physician group with 200+ members. Since 1995, Dr. Fotsch has led organizations that provide Internet-based healthcare applications, networks, and communications. Dr. Fotsch authored *Planning and Implementing Your Healthcare Internet Strategy,* published by Atlantic Information Services, and a chapter on eHealth liability in *Medical Malpractice, A Physician's Sourcebook* (2005 Humana Press Inc.). Dr. Fotsch is a member of several national committees on health information technology, including the JCAHO HIT Committee and the HL7 PHR Committee. He was the first recipient of the liability carrier annual Patient Safety Award in 2005. He is a frequent conference speaker in healthcare programs and is regularly quoted in the national press as an expert in physician Internet and IT issues.

—⁂—

[1] Markle Foundation, Connecting for Health, *The Personal Health Working Group, Final Report,* July 2003. Available at http://www.markle.org/downloadable_assets/final_phwg_report1.pdf (accessed April 2, 2007).

[2] Harris Interactive, "Two in Five Adults Keep Personal or Family Health Records and Almost Everybody Thinks This Is a Good Idea," news release, August 10, 2004. Available at http://www.harrisinteractive.com/news/allnewsbydate.asp?NewsID=832 (accessed April 6, 2007).

[3] Accenture, "Consumers See Electronic Health Records as Important Factor When Choosing a Physician and Are Willing to Pay for the Service, Accenture Research Finds," news release, February 26, 2007. Available at http://newsroom.accenture.com/article_display.cfm?article_id=4509 (accessed April 2, 2007).

[4] Markle Foundation, Connecting for Health, *The Personal Health Working Group, Final Report.*

[5] The National Committee on Vital and Health Statistics, *Personal Health Records and*

Personal Health Record Systems: A Report and Recommendations, February 2006. Available at http://www.hhs.gov/healthit/ahic/materials/meeting06/cemp/NCVHSPHRreport.pd f (accessed April 6, 2007).

[6] Institute of Medicine, Committee on Quality of Health Care in America, *To Err Is Human: Building a Safer Health System,* Linda T. Kohn, Janet M. Corrigan, and Molla S. Donaldson, eds. (Washington, D.C.: National Academy Press, 2000).

[7] Harris Interactive, "Two in Five Adults Keep Personal or Family Health Records and Almost Everybody Thinks This Is a Good Idea."

[8] Markle Foundation, Connecting for Health, *Connecting Americans to Their Healthcare: Final Report,* July 2004. Available at http://www.connectingforhealth.org/resources/wg_eis_final_report_0704.pdf (accessed April 6, 2007).

[9] Institute for the Future, *Executive Summary: Twenty-first Century Healthcare Consumers* (San Francisco: Jossey-Bass, 1998).

[10] The National Committee on Vital and Health Statistics, *Personal Health Records and Personal Health Record Systems: A Report and Recommendations.*

[11] Harris Interactive, "Two in Five Adults Keep Personal or Family Health Records and Almost Everybody Thinks This Is a Good Idea."

[12] Roy P. C. Kessels, "Patients' Memory for Medical Information," *Journal of the Royal Society of Medicine* 96 (May 2003): 219–22.

[13] Ronald C. Plotnikoff et al., "Efficacy of an E-mail Intervention for the Promotion of Physical Activity and Nutrition Behavior in the Workplace Context," *American Journal of Health Promotion* 19 (July/August 2005): 422.

[14] Institute of Medicine, Committee on Quality of Health Care in America, *To Err Is Human: Building a Safer Health System.*

[15] Markle Foundation, Connecting for Health, *Connecting Americans to Their Healthcare: Final Report.*

[16] Harris Interactive, "Patient/Physician Online Communication: Many Patients Want It, Would Pay for It, and It Would Influence Their Choice of Doctors and Health Plans," 2002. Available at http://www.harrisinteractive.com/news/newsletters/healthnews/HI_HealthCareNew s2002Vol2_Iss08.pdf (accessed April 2, 2007).

[17] S. E. Ross et al., "Providing a Web-based Online Medical Record with Electronic Communication Capabilities to Patients with Congestive Heart Failure: Randomized Trial," *Journal of Medical Internet Research* 6 (May 2004): e12. Abstract available at http://www.ncbi.nlm.nih.gov/entrez/query.fcgi?db=pubmed&cmd=Retrieve&dopt=A bstractPlus&list_uids=15249261&query_hl=1&itool=pubmed_docsum (accessed March 26, 2007).

[18] Victor M. Montori et al., "Telecare for Patients With Type 1 Diabetes and Inadequate Glycemic Control," *Diabetes Care* 27 (2004): 1088–94 and Leslie Lenert et al., "Automated E-mail Messaging as a Tool for Improving Quit Rates in an Internet Smoking Cessation Intervention," *Journal of the American Medical Informatics Association* 11, no. 4 (2004): 235–40.

[19] World Health Organization, *Adherence to Long-term Therapies: Evidence for Action,* 2003. Available at http://www.who.int/chp/knowledge/publications/adherence_report/en/index.html (accessed April 2, 2007).

[20] Centers for Disease Control and Prevention, National Center for Chronic Disease

Prevention & Health Promotion, *Behavioral Risk Factor Surveillance System: Trends Data, 1990–2002.* Available at http://apps.nccd.cdc.gov/brfss/Trends/trendchart.asp?qkey=10010&state=US (accessed April 2, 2007).

[21] Mayo Clinic, "Computerized Reminders Boost Mammography Screening Rates," news release, March 26, 2007. Available at http://www.mayoclinic.org/news2007-rst/3977.html (accessed April 2, 2007).

[22] D. F. Tate, E. H. Jackvony, and R. R. Wing, "Effects of Internet Behavioral Counseling on Weight Loss in Adults at Risk for Type 2 Diabetes: a Randomized Trial," *Journal of the American Medical Association,* 289, no. 14 (2003): 1833–36.

[23] Markle Foundation, Connecting for Health, *Connecting Americans to Their Healthcare: Final Report.*

[24] California HealthCare Foundation, *National Consumer Health Privacy Survey 2005,* November 2005. Executive summary available at http://chcf.org/documents/ihealth/ConsumerPrivacy2005ExecSum.pdf (accessed April 2, 2007).

CHAPTER 5

Leading the Way: Hospital Leadership in Health Information Technology

Richard J. Umbdenstock

—⚭—

Editor's Introduction

America's hospitals and physicians are at the forefront of modernizing healthcare through the use of information technology. Working with technology companies, hospitals are the leading innovators and largest investors in clinical IT systems, a market that is expected to reach nearly $5 billion annually by 2015.[1] The real-world experiences of thousands of hospitals across the country prove that when clinical processes are driven by health information technology, lives and money are saved.* Additionally, many health systems and hospitals have begun collaborating with other stakeholders, and even competitors, to build health information exchanges in their communities. Without a doubt, improving the delivery of care today and building a nationwide information network for tomorrow would not happen without the innovation and dedication of America's hospitals.

—⚭—

Every day, healthcare providers face urgent situations: an unidentified accident victim arrives unconscious and bleeding profusely; a toddler experiencing an apparent asthma attack is brought to the emergency department by a caregiver; a middle-aged male with a history of heart problems comes to the hospital with pain in his chest.

In all these situations, hospital staff must act fast to stabilize and treat the patient. However, their work can be hindered by a lack of information about the patient's medical history. Take the

---

* For real-world success stories of hospitals and health systems deploying health information technology, please see the white paper on the 2006 CHIME-CHT Transformational Leadership Award, presented by the College of Health Information Management Executives (CHIME) and the Center for Health Transformation. The paper is available at www.cio-chime.org and www.healthtransformation.net.

unconscious and unidentified accident victim: Hospital staff cannot ascertain anything about her medical history. Her general state of health—even her age—must be estimated as they work to treat her. The toddler is conscious, but she is too young to effectively answer questions from the medical staff. On the other hand, the heart patient is conscious and should be able to answer most of the medical staff's questions. But is his information reliable? Does he know the specifics of his last EKG results and the exact names and doses of all the medications he is taking?

In cases such as these, healthcare providers must make critical decisions with only limited or incomplete information to guide them, relying on their training and on care processes. Although the results are largely positive, quality and patient safety could be improved if complete patient information were available to all providers at the point of care.

Physicians treating patients with emergency conditions need three pieces of critical information:

(1) the current medications the patient is taking, including the dosage and frequency
(2) known allergies
(3) history of chronic illnesses, including recent treatments, tests, and disease management protocols

A fully integrated electronic health record system that instantly pulls data from healthcare providers across the spectrum of care—acute care hospitals, community physicians, therapists, pharmacies, ambulatory care centers, and others—would put this information at the caregiver's fingertips, undoubtedly leading to more informed care and better outcomes.

Current Hospital Health IT Use

Hospitals and health systems have made impressive strides in harnessing health information technology (IT) to improve patient care, quality, and efficiency. The field is now challenged to expand health IT use and integrate it into routine care processes in hospitals large and small, in both rural and urban areas. Hospitals stand on the brink of a new era in health information exchange. Continued advances in health IT could allow healthcare providers in and out of the hospital to share patient information electronically throughout the spectrum of patient care, alleviating many of the major challenges facing our healthcare system today, including the problem of fragmented information and delivery with multiple points of entry, multiple providers, and multiple payers.

Already, the use of electronic order-entry systems with clinical decision-support functions has been shown to reduce adverse drug events and medication errors. Medication bar-coding also has produced documented reductions in drug-related errors. In addition, health IT helps improve efficiency in healthcare delivery. Anecdotal evidence suggests that applications such as digital imaging software can decrease radiology costs, while order-entry medication functions have saved some hospitals and health systems substantial amounts of money by encouraging greater use of formulary drugs.

Health IT systems also are expected to save money and time for the healthcare system as a whole by lowering the incidence of repeated laboratory and radiology tests and improving outcomes. However, while healthcare providers may realize some financial efficiency from health IT, these savings are less than their costs. The return on investment, for the most part, will accrue more to payers and purchasers than to the providers paying for the systems.

Healthcare providers currently use many different kinds of IT, including clinical systems for maintaining records, tracking medications, and storing and viewing images. They also use IT systems for billing, scheduling and other administrative tasks. The most frequently discussed clinical applications are the electronic health record (EHR), which provides all of a patient's information through a single point of access, and computerized physician order-entry (CPOE) systems, which allow physicians to electronically order tests, consultations, and medications. CPOE systems also generally provide advice on best practices or alerts to possible adverse consequences, such as an allergy or a harmful drug interaction. Ideally, an EHR system will incorporate CPOE and other valuable functions, such as ways to view laboratory and radiological test results.

To gauge the extent of health IT use among hospitals and better understand the barriers to greater adoption, the American Hospital

Association (AHA) surveyed community hospitals in 2005 and 2006.[2] More than 900 hospitals responded in 2005 and more than 1,500 hospitals—nearly a third of all community hospitals in the United States—did so in 2006. In both years, the respondents were representative of all community hospitals by size, location, and teaching status.

According to the survey results, hospitals realize the potential of health IT to improve the safety and quality of care. Despite significant financial and implementation challenges, hospitals are making considerable progress in health IT adoption, with 68 percent reporting fully or partially implemented EHRs in 2006. The 11 percent with fully

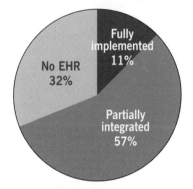

More than Two-thirds of Hospitals Had Fully or Partially Implemented EHRs in 2006

An EHR integrates electonically originated and maintained patient-level clinical health information, derived from multiple sources, into one point of access. An EHR replaces the paper medical record as the primary source of patient information.

Spectrum of IT Use

	Getting Started	Low	Moderate	High
Level of Use	0-3 Functions (0-25%) Fully Implemented	4-7 Functions (26-50%) Fully Implemented	8-11 Functions (51-75%) Fully Implemented	12-15 Functions (76-100%) Fully Implemented
Functions	• Access to current medical records • Access to medical history • Access to patient flow sheets • Access to patient demographics • Order-entry—lab • Results review—lab	• Order-entry—radiology • Results review—radiology images (incl. PACS) • Results review—radiology report • Results review—consultant report • Order-entry—pharmacy		• Real-time drug interaction alerts • Back-end drug interaction alerts • Clinical guidelines and pathways • Patient support through home monitoring, self-testing, and interactive patient education

implemented EHRs were more likely to be large, urban, and/or teaching hospitals.

The level of EHR use varies with many different hospital characteristics, particularly size. As capacity increases, so does use of EHRs. While 23 percent of responding hospitals with 500 or more beds had fully implemented EHRs in 2006—and 92 percent had fully or partially implemented EHRs—only 3 percent of hospitals with 50 or fewer beds had fully implemented EHRs. Among the smallest hospitals, 55 percent have no EHRs. Similarly, urban hospitals, teaching hospitals, and those that were part of a hospital system were more likely to have implemented EHRs in 2006. Financial status also helps determine a hospital's level of IT use; hospitals with positive margins had greater IT use.

The Evolutionary Nature of Health IT Use

Implementing an EHR system requires significant changes and improvements to clinical and administrative work processes. Beyond the technological changes, physicians, nurses, and other hospital staff must integrate new ways of processing, storing, and retrieving the information they use every minute of every day. Not all implementations are successful, and failure is very expensive. Given the large-scale changes—and large-scale costs—many hospitals are taking an incremental approach. For example, they may first implement IT systems in ancillary departments that serve the entire hospital, such

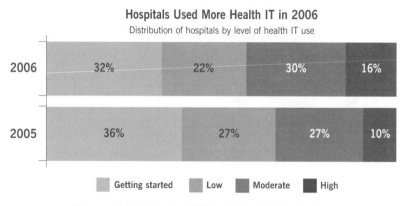

Hospitals Used More Health IT in 2006

Distribution of hospitals by level of health IT use

2006	32%	22%	30%	16%
2005	36%	27%	27%	10%

Getting started ■ Low ■ Moderate ■ High

Difference in distribution from 2005 to 2006 statistically significant at p<01.

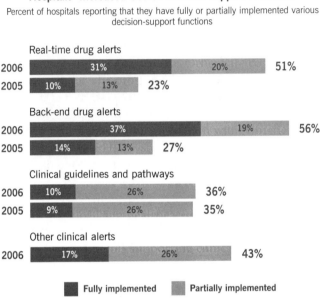

Hospitals' Increased Use of Decision-support Functions

Percent of hospitals reporting that they have fully or partially implemented various decision-support functions

Real-time drug alerts

2006   31%   20%   **51%**
2005   10%   13%   **23%**

Back-end drug alerts

2006   37%   19%   **56%**
2005   14%   13%   **27%**

Clinical guidelines and pathways

2006   10%   26%   **36%**
2005   9%   26%   **35%**

Other clinical alerts

2006   17%   26%   **43%**

■ Fully implemented   ■ Partially implemented

as the pharmacy or laboratory, working over time to connect them. Others may implement systems department by department.

To capture the diversity and incremental nature of health IT use among hospitals, the survey asked about distinct clinical functions, such as reviewing lab results or ordering drugs electronically. AHA created four groups of use based on the number of EHR functions that were reported to be *fully implemented* at each surveyed hospital, ranging from just getting started to having almost all the functions in place.

In 2006, 46 percent of community hospitals reported moderate or high use of health IT, compared to 37 percent in 2005. Sixteen percent of hospitals had implemented almost all the functions in 2006, up from 10 percent in 2005. Despite this growth in the upper end of the spectrum, more than half of hospitals were still in the "getting started" or "low" use groups in 2006.

Hospitals also reported dramatic increases in the use of computerized alerts to prevent negative drug interactions and other decision-support tools. In 2006, more than half of hospitals used drug interaction alerts—a key element for improving medication safety—compared to 23 percent in 2005. Use of electronic clinical guidelines and pathways that support physicians in making clinical decisions, such as which diagnostic tests or medications may be appropriate for a given condition, also grew.

Challenges to Hospital Health IT Adoption

Health IT is expensive. Spending will depend on both hospital size and the technologies selected. Often, health IT systems require multi-year investments, and hospitals generally find that the operating costs for clinical IT systems grow annually as they implement more systems and deploy additional functions.

Cost was cited by hospitals as the greatest challenge to increased health IT use in both years, with 94 percent of hospitals surveyed in 2006 saying that the initial costs were a "significant barrier" or "somewhat of a barrier" to health IT adoption. The ongoing costs of maintaining and upgrading IT systems also present concerns, with 87 percent of hospitals citing them as a barrier.

Lack of interoperability between current health IT systems also poses a challenge. To have data at the point of care, laboratory information systems must be integrated with pharmacy systems and radiology systems, as well as with the patient's health record. Currently, hospitals devote considerable staff and financial resources to creating interfaces between systems or other IT "workarounds" and to managing these interfaces. Health IT adoption would be greatly facilitated by standardization across information technologies, as increased interoperability decreases the need for—and expense of—interfaces. In addition, the current generation of health IT does not always meet the needs of clinicians in terms of comprehensiveness, ease of use, and speed.

Making the transition from a paper-based to an electronic system is very difficult. Work processes must not only be automated, but ideally should be reviewed and re-engineered to ensure that broken or insufficient processes are fixed. This level of care transformation is time-consuming and involves numerous staff from across the hospital, including IT personnel, physicians, nurses, ancillary providers, etc.

While hospitals work hard at managing these changes, there is no guarantee that the majority of personnel will properly utilize the expensive new IT system once it becomes operable. There recently have been several high-profile incidents in which physicians and nurses have balked at the introduction of new IT systems. In some cases, the clinical staff rejected the new system, and the hospital was forced to take it offline and rework its design. In other cases, staff members who are uncomfortable using an IT system, or feel the system does not meet their needs, may not formally reject the system, but instead develop their own workarounds, limiting the efficacy of the organization's investment.

Hospitals also must compete for scarce IT personnel, without whom they cannot build and manage complex IT systems. The number of trained IT professionals, particularly those with expertise in healthcare IT systems, is not meeting the overwhelming demand. In 2001 the U.S. Bureau of Labor Statistics projected a 49 percent growth in the number of health IT workers by the end of the decade. However, according to an American Health Information Management Association report, that estimate did not account for the accelerated push for EHRs throughout the nation.[3] The dearth of IT personnel has ramifications that extend beyond building and maintaining the systems—hospitals will be unable to train clinical and administrative staff to use the systems to the full extent of their capabilities.

Health IT in Action

Despite the numerous challenges, many organizations have implemented extensive and successful systems. Partners HealthCare System in Boston, Massachusetts, is one example.

Founded in 1994, the system has been at the forefront of health IT, already exceeding national projections for health IT use by end of the decade. CPOE is fully implemented at both Brigham and Women's and Massachusetts General Hospitals, as well as at two of Partners' four acute-care hospitals. The system hopes to bring the remaining hospitals online by the end of 2007. Partners is also a leader in the use of EHRs: 85 to 90 percent of physicians at the two academic medical centers and about 70 percent of community primary care physicians in the Partners network currently use or are implementing EHRs. In addition, Partners' patients also have access to their own personal medical records through the system.

The benefits of Partners' investment in health IT have been substantial. Studies of Brigham and Women's Hospital's CPOE system, which utilizes a decision-support function, found medication errors were reduced by 80 percent, with serious medication errors reduced by 55 percent. Further studies of CPOE throughout the system found a significant reduction in inappropriate antibiotic use, increased appropriateness of medication and radiology procedure orders, significantly faster physician notification of patient test results, and an overall reduction in patient length of stay. Additional studies found that with reminders embedded in the EHR system, patients with chronic conditions received recommended care more frequently—a 30 percent increase for diabetic patients and a 25 percent increase for patients with coronary artery disease. Overall, Partners noted that the order-entry function of its EHR system has led to medication orders being switched to lower-cost but equally effective drugs 15 percent of the time.[4]

Connecting Care

There are clear benefits to using health IT in the hospital, but even greater benefits can be realized through a "wired" system in which health information can be made available to the right person at the right time to inform clinical care. Imagine the advantages if an emergency department were able to access on arrival a patient's medications and medical history, or if an inpatient hospital were able to call up the most recent test results and records for a patient transferred from a nursing home. The transition back to post–acute care settings also would be eased by electronic information-sharing.

A 2005 RAND Corporation study estimated that improved efficiency through the use of health IT in both inpatient and outpatient care would result in $77 billion in annual savings.[5] A second 2005 study led by researchers from the Center for Information Technology Leadership endorsed this estimate.[6] These savings were directly attributable to reduced length of stay, reduced administrative time on the part of nursing staff, and more efficient drug utilization. According to RAND, increased use of health IT, particularly the introduction of CPOE systems, would dramatically improve patient safety. If all hospitals utilized CPOE systems, RAND estimated that about 200,000 adverse drug events per year could be averted, at an annual savings of $1 billion. However, RAND also noted that most of the financial benefits would accrue to payers and purchasers of care, not to the providers who must invest in the systems.

Information Exchange Efforts Under Way

Health information exchange (HIE) efforts are under way in communities across the country. HIE projects vary widely, but generally involve diverse stakeholders joining together to plan, finance, and implement systems to share electronic health information across care settings. Hospitals are serving as a driving force behind most of them. In one survey of HIE projects, hospitals were part of the governance structure in more than 60 percent of cases. In addition, hospitals often provide financial support. While these projects are known by many names, they are increasingly referred to as regional health information organizations (RHIOs).

As described in a subsequent chapter of this book, Inland Northwest Health Services (INHS) is one example of a RHIO that is improving the health of its community. A 501(c)3 not-for-profit corporation, INHS was created by four competing hospital systems and now serves parts of Washington, Idaho, California, Montana, Oregon, Alaska, and Canada. The network includes 38 hospitals with more than 4,400 beds, sharing electronic health information on more than 2 million patients. Inpatient hospital, laboratory, and image data can be viewed at more than 50 clinics and 400 physician offices. The network also supports a telehealth program connected to 76 hospitals, clinics, and public health agencies throughout its primarily rural service area. INHS participants have seen a variety of benefits from their participation in the system, including a significant reduction in medical errors.

In 2006, the AHA commissioned a study exploring the risks, benefits, and lessons learned for hospitals and health systems contemplating or engaging in HIE initiatives in their communities.[7] The study urged hospital and health system executives to be proactive, letting clinical and care improvements drive the project. HIE is becoming more of a reality; as one executive noted, "Hoping it will go away is not a good strategy."

Finally, the study also cautioned executives to carefully consider their internal capabilities, as well as the risks and benefits of being a leader, before engaging in a new HIE effort. Taking part in an HIE effort may not be right for every organization at this point. However, the rewards for pioneers could be immense.

Barriers to Health Information Exchange

Health information exchange is still in its infancy, but momentum is certainly building. To date, more than 160 HIE projects have been launched across the country, touching nearly every state and many communities. However, many challenges remain.

Like health IT adoption, HIE financially benefits other stake-holders more than it does the providers holding the data. As a result, outside funding is sought in many cases. Many HIE projects have begun with grant funding through federal or state governments. For example, the Agency for Healthcare Research and Quality has provided more than $100 million in funding, and the state of New York recently announced $53 million in grants to support health IT projects throughout the state.

Many providers, including hospitals, may be reluctant to share their patients' clinical information with other organizations for legal or competitive reasons. However, healthcare information cannot be regarded as the property of any individual organization. Improved clinical care will be realized when the right information is available to the right provider—whomever it might be—at the right time to be used for patient care. Achieving that goal requires that the data not belong to an individual organization, physician, or vendor, but that it can be exchanged to support clinical care. Limiting use of shared data to providers in the course of treatment may help allay privacy concerns as well as issues stemming from competitive business strategies.

Patient health information is subject to a wide variety of local, state, and federal privacy and security laws, most notably the Health Insurance Portability and Accountability Act of 1996 (HIPAA). Hospitals have worked diligently to ensure the privacy and security of patients' health information. However, the multiplicity of privacy and security laws and rules issued by accrediting bodies makes compliance difficult and can interfere with patient care.

Any HIE endeavor must ensure public trust. In an age of identity theft and insecurity regarding health coverage, keeping health information confidential is vital. But sharing health information requires matching records across providers, and, at the moment, hospitals and other providers do not have a unique key for matching patients and their records. The safety and quality risks of missing information or matching patients to the wrong record are serious at best and deadly at worst. Furthermore, to realize the benefits of HIE, physicians must be able to trust that the data is accurate, or they will not use it. Therefore, a single mechanism for matching patients and their records is needed. One possibility is a health information authentication number used only for care delivery and protected by privacy and security provisions. These numbers would allow patients to be matched to their records with certainty. They would also promote privacy by allowing patient identification information, such as Social Security numbers, to be removed from health records.

Stark and Anti-kickback Laws

Other federal laws and regulations further impede health IT adoption. As we have demonstrated, to realize health IT's full promise, information must be shared across patient care settings, including physicians' offices. Many physicians, however, do not have the financial or technical resources needed to navigate the complex health IT market. While not all are in a position to do so, some hospitals may want to provide community physicians with hardware, software, connectivity, or other assistance that would allow them to maintain EHRs for their patients and share clinical data with the hospital.

In a fully wired health system, the need for hospitals to provide good electronic data to physicians will be akin to providing a well-stocked and smoothly functioning operating room. When hospitals and health systems directly or indirectly fund IT systems for physicians, however, they encounter significant barriers imposed by physician self-referral laws, often called Stark laws, as well as anti-kickback laws.

Spearheaded in the late 1980s and early 1990s by Congressman Fortney "Pete" Stark (D-California), the Stark laws established an enforceable rule against physician "self-referrals" in order to avoid any negative impact that a physician's economic interest in an entity might have on decisions about a patient's healthcare needs. Like that of the Stark laws, the main purpose of the federal anti-kickback law, enacted in 1972, is to protect patients and the federal healthcare programs from fraudulent and abusive claims. Despite having similar purposes, the Stark and anti-kickback laws are two separate statutes with different compliance requirements.

Stark laws prohibit a physician from referring Medicare and Medicaid patients for certain designated health services to an entity if the physician, or a member of the physician's immediate family, has a financial relationship with that entity. The anti-kickback law makes it a felony for anyone to knowingly and willfully give a physician anything of value, either money or non-monetary items of value, in exchange for a referral. It is likewise illegal for physicians to ask for or receive anything of value in exchange for a referral.

Both CMS and OIG published final rules on August 8, 2006, to provide some regulatory protections for health IT donations. In response to comments from the hospital field and others, the final rules offer more flexibility than those the agencies proposed in the fall of 2005 and will protect donations of a broad range of health IT resources, such as software, interfaces, connectivity services, training, and help-desk and other types of maintenance and support services.

While the final rules provide more flexibility, they include several limitations and requirements. For example, to be protected from penalties, any software that is donated must be interoperable. This requirement raises some practical questions, since true interoperability does not yet exist, and it will take some time to understand how hospitals and other possible donors will respond to the regulatory changes. The workability and impact on rates of physician adoption of EHRs remain to be seen.

Looking Ahead

The federal government has prioritized both the adoption of EHRs and the development of a Nationwide Health Information Network (NHIN) that would allow clinical data to follow the patient across care settings. The AHA strongly supports the growing focus on the use of health IT in improving patient safety and quality care in our hospitals. As Congress and the administration consider ways to encourage adoption and greater information exchange, the AHA will advocate for solutions that address the major barriers to realizing the promise of health IT, including:

- *Increased Standardization:* Both adoption and information-sharing will increase when health information and IT applications are built on open, interoperable standards.

- *Funding:* Providers and payers both must contribute to covering the costs of health IT investment and maintenance.

- *Regulatory Relief:* Meaningful changes to the Stark and anti-kickback laws are needed to facilitate information-sharing between hospitals and physician offices.

- *A Single Set of Privacy and Security Laws:* A single set of national rules is needed to facilitate the use of health IT and to ensure access by healthcare providers to information at the point of care.

- *A Uniform Approach to Matching Patients to Their Records:* A single patient authentication number is needed to prevent serious medical and safety errors.

This is an exciting time for the hospital field. Health information technology holds great promise for improving quality, patient safety, and efficiency of healthcare. Working together, healthcare and government leaders can realize that promise and help propel our nation's hospitals into the electronic information age.

—⚏—

Richard J. Umbdenstock is President and Chief Executive Officer of the American Hospital Association (AHA) and a past chair of the AHA's Board of Trustees. Prior to joining the AHA, he was executive vice president of Providence Health & Services in Spokane, Washington. Mr. Umbdenstock's career includes 11 years as an independent consultant for voluntary hospital governing boards in the United States and Canada. On the AHA Board, he chaired the Operations Committee and the Task Force on Coverage & Access, was an ex-officio member of Regional Policy Board 9, and served on the Circle of Life Committee. A diplomate of ACHE, he received a B.A. in Politics in 1972 from Fairfield University, Fairfield, Connecticut, and an M.S. in Health Services Administration in 1974 from the State University of

New York at Stony Brook. In May 2003 he was awarded a Doctor of Laws honorary degree from Gonzaga University in Spokane, Washington.

—◊◊◊—

[1] Lynne A. Dunbrack, Scott Lundstrom, and Ted Dangson, *U.S. Electronic Health Records 2005: 2015 Spending Forecast and Analysis,* Health Industry Insights report, July 2006.

[2] American Hospital Association, *Forward Momentum: Hospital Use of Information Technology,* October 2005. Available at http://www.aha.org/aha/content/2005/pdf/FINALNonEmbITSurvey105.pdf (accessed April 6, 2007).

[3] American Health Information Management Association and American Medical Informatics Association, *Building the Workforce for Health Information Transformation,* February 2006. Available at http://www.ahima.org/emerging_issues/Workforce_web.pdf (accessed April 6, 2007).

[4] Testimony of John Glaser, Ph.D., Vice President and Chief Information Officer, Partners HealthCare, before the Subcommittee on Technology, Innovation and Competitiveness of the Senate Committee on Commerce, Science and Transportation, "Use of Information Technology to Improve the Quality of Patient Care," June 30, 2005.

[5] RAND Corporation, *Health Information Technology: Can HIT Lower Costs and Improve Quality?* 2005. Available at http://www.rand.org/pubs/research_briefs/RB9136/index1.html (accessed April 4, 2007).

[6] J. Walker et al., "The Value of Health Care Information Exchange and Interoperability," *Health Affairs Web Exclusive,* January 19, 2005. Available at http://content.healthaffairs.org/cgi/content/abstract/hlthaff.w5.10v1?maxtoshow=&HITS=10&hits=10&RESULTFORMAT=&author1=Jan+Walker&andorexactfulltext=and&searchid=1&FIRSTINDEX=0&resourcetype=HWCIT (accessed March 28, 2007).

[7] American Hospital Association, *Health Information Exchange Projects: What Hospitals and Health Systems Need to Know,* April 2006. Available at http://www.aha.org/aha/content/2006/pdf/AHARHIOfinal.pdf (accessed April 6, 2007).

CHAPTER 6

Best Demonstrated Practices in Ambulatory Care: Driving Adoption of Electronic Health Records

Glen E. Tullman

—ɯ—

Editor's Introduction

The majority of all healthcare in America is delivered in the ambulatory care setting. In 2004, more than 910 million visits were made to ambulatory physician offices.[1] That's an average of three visits for every American. Unfortunately, most of the care we receive in the typical physician's office is delivered using a paper medical record. But things are changing. A recent survey by the American Academy of Family Physicians shows that adoption of health information technology in family medicine has grown to more than a third of all family physicians, up from 10 percent in 2003. The American Medical Group Association notes that 80 percent of all group practices have invested in electronic health records, electronic prescribing, and other technologies. All these doctors, be they solo practitioners or large systems like Intermountain Healthcare, are delivering better patient care and doing so more efficiently because their clinical processes are driven by health information technology. They are truly pioneers, as the current system is not designed to encourage health IT adoption. From a system-wide perspective, the current rate of adoption is insufficient. We must make radical changes, with fundamental payment reform being most important, so that the adoption of technology is the norm and not the exception.

—ɯ—

I did not grow up in the healthcare industry, nor am I a physician by training or education. So when I arrived in healthcare nine years ago, I had to ask a lot of questions—questions that led to a lot of listening and learning.

The healthcare environment I encountered was replete with myths, misaligned incentives, and conflict. The only facts that anyone could agree on were that the system was broken and that patients were paying the price, both in terms of quality of care and high costs. Meanwhile, innovation was being stifled by several commonly held beliefs: that hospitals would drive the necessary changes that could repair the system; that physicians did not like and would not use technology; that healthcare was somehow different from other industries; and that healthcare was a zero-sum game, requiring the winner to take something away from another healthcare stakeholder.

As it turns out, each of these "facts" is a myth. I'll address each one head-on:

- Given that physicians control 80 percent of the spending decisions in healthcare, it follows that real change must begin with them, not with hospitals. In fact, the system that is evolving will reward physicians for helping patients stay healthy and keeping them out of hospitals.

- Physicians do not resist technology; they resist technologies that fail to save them time or money or do not improve quality.

- In the area of technology, we can indeed learn from other industries. Healthcare and education, the two sectors with the smallest investment in information technology, are our most troubled.

- When we are open to the lessons of other industries, we discover that healthcare is not a zero-sum game after all. Instead, using technology to inform and connect physicians and other healthcare professionals is the key to a winning solution for *all* the stakeholders in the healthcare system.

More and more people are beginning to understand that many of healthcare's commonly held beliefs are in fact just myths, and that we must follow every other sector in our economy and adopt information technology to facilitate real change. I believe that two technologies, both available today, are the key: electronic prescribing, considered to be the on-ramp to the electronic healthcare highway, and the electronic health record (EHR), which not only automates common physician behaviors like charge capture and documentation, but also arms physicians with the latest information and can connect them to the rest of the stakeholders in healthcare.

Despite the clear benefits of adoption, and much to the chagrin of everyone who has an interest in improving healthcare, physicians simply have not invested in health information technology at the pace one would expect. Today, some 80 percent of physicians still run their practices with paper medical records.

The explanation for physicians' relatively low EHR adoption rate has more to do with myth than reality. Many so-called "first-generation" EHR vendors sold large software systems primarily to hospitals, and were not successful in gaining widespread utilization or realizing significant transformation. What was needed was software that physicians not only needed to have, but also wanted to use. These first-generation systems largely failed in that regard, and when the software was taken into high-volume ambulatory settings, the problem became even more apparent.

What the hospitals and many physicians failed to see is that EHR adoption is not just about the software—it is about making it work. As Thomas Edison said, "Nothing that's good works by itself just to please you. You've got to make the damn thing work." In the case of the EHR, making it work has more to do with the process of skillful deployment and building full utilization than with the technology itself. To get physicians to undergo the change process, you have to convince them, not tell them.

How do you convince them? Conventional wisdom assumes that physicians will be motivated to adopt a new technology if they are convinced it adheres to best practices and will enhance patient safety or raise the quality of care they provide. Unfortunately, the best-practices argument assumes that patients are *unsafe* under current practices. While there are clear variances and disparities in care, medical errors, and other serious problems, blaming physicians for system-wide dysfunctions is hardly the best way to encourage them to change their behavior. A better approach is to capitalize on the scientific training of physicians, who are taught to trust what they can see and repeat. Physicians want to see the evidence and to be assured it will work.

So let's give them exactly what they want: best *demonstrated* practices. Rather than ask physicians to trust a hypothetical argument, we must demonstrate the benefits of the technology with evidence from other physicians' practices. From best *demonstrated* practices, physicians can not only see firsthand how others have successfully implemented EHRs, but they can also learn valuable lessons that will help them rapidly deploy the technology to solve everyday problems.

The Information Bottleneck

In healthcare, as in other information-intensive industries, the fundamental problem is that clinicians lack quick, reliable access to the information they need at the point of care. The centuries-old practice of storing medical records on paper makes information almost impossible to access in a timely manner and makes it susceptible to loss, misplacement, or error. Paper-based recordkeeping also precludes the use of modern information technology to coordinate care, routinely measure quality, or reduce costly medical errors.

The answer to this information bottleneck, as other industries have discovered, is the delivery of "just right, just-in-time information." The banking industry, perhaps earlier than any other, discovered how to use technology to deliver "just right" information with the Automated Teller Machine. Today, anyone with a bank account can use an ATM in New York, Paris, or Hong Kong to transfer money across currencies and continents in a matter of seconds. In a world where such technological marvels are possible, you might be excused for wondering why 80 percent of physicians—who every day deal in life and death—still lack instant access at the point of care to their patient's medication histories and clinical records.

The impact of the information bottleneck on the quality of patient care is profound. To mention just one example, the Institute of Medicine (IOM) estimates that 1.5 million Americans are harmed each year by medication errors, and that thousands die as a result.[2] Mistakes in drug delivery are so widespread that, on average, a hospitalized patient is subject to at least one medication error per day.

As a solution, the IOM called for all prescriptions to be written electronically by 2010. Specifically, the IOM recommended that physicians use interoperable electronic prescription and clinical decision-support software, such as that available in the best EHRs, with point-of-care reference information accessed via the Internet.

Using such an interoperable EHR system, a patient's drug information would follow him or her from the doctor's office to the hospital to the pharmacy, avoiding many of the "hand-off errors" common today.

To that end, Allscripts, along with Microsoft, Google, Dell, WellPoint, and others, is leading the National ePrescribing Patient Safety Initiative (NEPSI). The goal of NEPSI is to provide safe, easy, and secure electronic prescribing technology to every physician in the country—at no cost. More information can be found at www.nationalerx.com.

Bottleneck Economics

The healthcare information bottleneck also contributes to the high cost of care. According to the Centers for Medicare and Medicaid Services (CMS), overall spending on healthcare in the United States will top $2.2 trillion in 2006, making the U.S. healthcare industry arguably the world's largest, most inefficient business, based on cost-to-quality metrics. According to a comprehensive 2003 study by RAND, widespread adoption of interoperable EHRs could dramatically lower healthcare costs by producing efficiency and safety savings of between $142 and $371 billion.[3]

On the efficiency side, the study estimated the largest savings would come from increased utilization of cheaper generic medications and lower labor costs resulting from the automation of labor-intensive processes such as transcribing doctor's notes, responding to prescription refill requests, and creating, storing, and retrieving paper records. On the safety side, the study estimated savings of more than $150 billion a year from reduced medication errors, improved preventive services, and better management of chronic disease.

Demonstrated Best Practices and Common Barriers to EHR Adoption

Implementing an electronic health record is a serious undertaking that requires foresight, care, and planning—but it is by no means impossible. In fact, what is not well appreciated is that hundreds of physician groups—totaling thousands of doctors—have already implemented EHRs, and they are reaping significant rewards. In choosing to implement the systems, these practices had to overcome two primary barriers to adoption that show up again and again in physician surveys:

- The fear that the electronic health record will cost too much to implement and will produce little or no financial return on investment (ROI)

- The fear that physicians will find it so difficult to use the electronic health record that their productivity (and therefore, their incomes) will fall significantly

One important lesson about change in other industries is that reference sites and success stories can not only address the fear but may also create competitive energy that can help to accelerate progress. In that spirit, we have provided a sampling of practices of all sizes and backgrounds—from large to small, multi-specialty to academic, rural to urban—that succeeded beyond their expectations in overcoming the perceived barriers to EHR adoption. Today they are more profitable and better positioned that ever before.

Small Group Practice: North Fulton Family Medicine
Alpharetta and Cumming, Georgia

Dr. James Morrow, vice president of the eight-physician North Fulton Family Medicine practice, credits their EHR with saving his group $1 million in the first 18 months of operation—*after* accounting for the cost of implementation. The EHR has given the four-office practice instant access to patient records; eliminated the need for staff to locate, deliver, and re-file; saved time through notes that are created during the visit, rather than afterward; allowed for significant reductions in paperwork; and eliminated virtually all transcription costs. The recouped transcription costs alone have saved approximately $775,000 in the 18-month period.

The electronic health record also has freed up office space previously used for chart storage and sharply decreased the amount of time staff spend on administrative functions. In the first year of implementation alone, the practice eliminated $253,978 in labor costs associated with chart pulls, new patient chart generation, missing chart searches, transcription, lab result handling, and the coordination of referral letters. In total, the leadership of North Fulton concluded that the EHR saved them $33 per patient visit.

"The primary lesson we learned is, the sooner you implement an EMR [electronic medical record] system, the better off you will be," said Dr. Morrow, a recognized national authority on healthcare IT and winner of the prestigious HIMSS Davies Award. "Once you implement a system, you'll never want to go back to paper."

As for productivity losses due to implementation difficulties, they never materialized at North Fulton. Prior to implementation, the group consisted of four physicians treating 21,000 patients, with 3.5 support staff for every one clinician. Post-implementation, the practice has nearly tripled patient volume, while maintaining a 2.8 to 1 ratio of non-clinical to clinical staff, well below the national practice average. At the same time, per-patient costs fell by more than 10 percent. Overall, in the first year of electronic health record implementation, North Fulton's productivity, as measured by patient visits per provider, increased by 38.5 percent.

Small Group Specialty Practice: Atlantic Orthopedic
Wilmington, North Carolina
Atlantic Orthopedics is one of the largest general and sub-specialty orthopedic medicine groups in the Southeast, with a new musculoskeletal center and four satellite offices staffed by 11 surgeons, six physician assistants, and four physical therapists. The group's electronic health record has delivered significant economic benefits while solving one of its most vexing and expensive problems—the disappearing chart.

"We don't ever have a lost chart now because it's electronic," said Dr. Mark Rodger, a senior Atlantic surgeon. "So the old days of having to see a patient without a chart are gone." Having patient medical records and automated decision-making at their fingertips, no matter where they are, has enabled the group's physicians to provide higher-quality care, said Dr. Rodger, who often accesses the EHR from home when he consults with other physicians' patients while on call.

Besides delivering vastly improved connectivity and enhanced clinical decision-making, the EHR has dramatically reduced costs, according to Richard Truax, executive director of the practice. Atlantic has reduced transcription costs, significantly cut staffing for chart creation and filing, saved staff time lost searching for charts, streamlined billing and claims submissions, and eliminated the need for space and equipment to store charts. According to a rigorous ROI analysis that Truax conducted himself, the EHR will save Atlantic Orthopedics nearly $20,000 per physician annually.

On the productivity front, Truax took careful measures to avoid slowing Atlantic's physicians down. He chose an electronic health record with modular architecture, which enables individual Atlantic physicians to adopt one or a few modules of the full system first, get comfortable with the technology, and then add more functionality over time, at their own pace. The result, Truax says, is that "physician productivity didn't drop one iota."

Medium-Size Multi-Specialty: Affinity Medical Group
Tifton, Georgia

Affinity Health Group, a multi-specialty, 27-physician group in rural south Georgia, used a strict cost-benefit model to document the net benefits from its electronic health record—a startling one-year savings of $2.5 million and nearly $12.7 million over five years. Ray Cross, Affinity's chief executive officer, took one look at the numbers and decided they were too good to be true. "I gave them back to the business office, saying they certainly are wrong. There's no way these numbers are right," Cross recalled. "A few days later I got a call from our CFO, who's not an employee, saying, 'When you presented me with those numbers I didn't think that they could be right. But I ran them myself and they're even better.' We never had any idea we would save this kind of money."

Implementation of the electronic health record allowed Affinity to cut or reassign several positions directly related to the old paper record. Savings also came through reductions in transcription expenses. Before implementation of the EHR, caregivers dictated notes that other employees transcribed into the paper record. To avoid creating a dual-charge system, in which charges would be determined by both the paper record and the EHR, Affinity pre-loaded critical portions of the paper record into the electronic health record and then closed the paper chart the day the system went live.

As a result, Affinity reduced monthly transcription hours by 50 percent, enabling the elimination of four transcription positions.

Productivity losses during Affinity's implementation proved to be minimal. The practice budgeted for a 30 percent reduction in office visits due to the expected high learning curve, but the actual reduction was a mere 5 percent, with the rate of visits returning to normal in less than one month.

Large Multi-Specialty Group: Central Utah Clinic
Provo, Utah
Central Utah Clinic is the largest independent multi-specialty physician practice in Utah, with 78 physicians and 11 clinics providing care to rural communities throughout the state. One year after implementing an electronic health record, CUC conducted a study that revealed direct reductions in spending and increases in revenue of more than $952,000 compared to the previous year. CUC anticipates cumulative savings of more than $8.5 million over the next five years.

Savings were achieved due to reduced expenditures in areas directly related to the EHR's implementation: reduced transcription costs; reductions in staff required for pulling, filing, and maintaining charts; elimination of the cost of building charts for new patients; decreased physical space requirements due to a paperless record; and increased revenue due to improved documentation.

"We paid for the electronic health record within the first year," said Jamie Steck, CUC's director of information technology. "Not many companies or clinics of our size can say that. To save a million dollars in the first year—and our five-year projection is over $8.5 million—it's a no-lose situation."

Large Multi-Specialty Group: Southwest Medical Associates
Las Vegas, Nevada
Southwest Medical Associates (SMA) is the largest multi-specialty physician group in Nevada, with 250 physicians in 14 locations. A subsidiary of Sierra Health Services, the state's largest managed care organization, SMA aims to deliver the highest-quality patient care in the most cost-effective manner possible. In 2003, SMA implemented an electronic health record with electronic prescribing capabilities

designed to enhance care and save money by automating routine clinical tasks and enabling physicians to prescribe more low-cost generic medications.

After three years of using the system, SMA's generic fill rate has achieved a 4.8-percentage-point difference over a control group of physicians in other Sierra-owned groups that do not use electronic prescribing. SMA's increased generic utilization saves the group $4.75 million each year, or 7.2 percent of its 2005 drug spending of $66 million, which translates into savings for their covered patients. The electronic health record also greatly streamlines the process of approving prescription refills, in the process creating indirect financial savings of $208,640 a year through increased nurse productivity.

A key best practice emerged from SMA's decision to modify its bonus policy by mandating that only prescribing physicians who were 100 percent EHR-compliant would be eligible to receive bonuses. Within one month of making the change, 90 percent of all prescriptions written at SMA were electronic. By the end of two months, every SMA physician was using the EHR to prescribe medications and the practice now averages more than 80,000 electronic scripts per month, making it one of the highest-volume eRx groups in the nation.

Dr. Craig Morrow, the medical director of SMA who led the implementation, said the EHR has also delivered quality improvements. "Our physicians are convinced that the system's clinical decision support and automatic drug utilization review prevents medical errors that would previously have slipped by unnoticed. We've definitely seen a sharp decrease in errors since we began using the electronic health record."

Large Academic Medical Group: The George Washington University Medical Faculty Associates
Washington, D.C.

The George Washington University Medical Faculty Associates (MFA), the capital's largest multi-specialty group practice, experienced net savings of more than $2 million in the first year after implementation of an electronic health record. Savings came from sharply reduced transcription costs, staffing reductions of 20 full-time employees in the medical records department, and improved identification of diagnostic procedures. MFA estimates five-year savings from the EHR will amount to more than $11 million.

"This has been a home run," said Stephen Badger, CEO of Medical Faculty Associates, who applied expertise drawn from his experience outside healthcare. "We've seen an improvement in care, which was our key priority and focus, but at the same time we've accomplished an overall, measurable reduction in costs. We've transformed our business using software and technology, which is common outside healthcare but was, at least when we started to implement the electronic health record, seen as a unique accomplishment."

MFA also set a new standard for rapid EHR implementation and established a demonstrated best practice for overcoming another perceived barrier to adoption of electronic health records: the myth of the prolonged roll-out of a fully functional system. In a peer-reviewed article for the *Journal of Health Information Management,* Badger and MFA's clinical and IT executives described the rapid implementation process in a complex, academic setting that went live with 99 physicians and 130 residents and interns in just 28 days.[4] The deployment plan incorporated four critical strategies:

(1) Leveraging a "leadership triad," consisting of the senior lead ership from the physician, information technology, and executive areas of the practice
(2) Utilizing existing call-response protocols in the practice's call center to develop new electronic workflows that could be facilitated by the EHR
(3) Introducing "just-in-time training," a phased training strate gy that took physicians "live" on the EHR in their own work space immediately following classroom training sessions
(4) Inducing the "Eureka Effect" to overcome physician resist ance by highlighting small, quick wins and focusing on the EHR's ability to dramatically simplify daily tasks

As each of these best demonstrated practices shows the two primary barriers to the adoption of an electronic health record, perceived cost and productivity losses, are more myth than reality. With the right leadership and the right vendor partner, an electronic health record can indeed quickly produce enough ROI to offset its cost. Moreover, the deployment, properly planned and incorporating best practices, need not result in a loss of physician productivity or income. That should be encouraging news for any practice that has been seriously considering adopting the latest information technology to enhance care and lower costs.

But as great as these accomplishments are, I can't stop there. As Dr. Jerry Miller, founder and CEO of Holston Medical Group, says, "If all we do is provide world-class patient care to patients who walk through our doors, we'll be out of business in five years." Dr. Miller is no pessimist—far from it—though his comment is an acknowledgment of the difficult challenges facing medicine today, with costs on the rise and reimbursements falling. Holston Medical Group, a 102-physician multi-specialty group in Kingsport, Tennessee, is not where you might expect to find one of the leading and most innovative practices in the nation. But under Dr. Miller's leadership, Holston has become a powerful model for the future of healthcare in America.

The recipe for Holston's success, and for the success of every medical group in America, can be summarized in just two words: leadership and innovation. Under Dr. Miller's leadership, Holston Medical Group has leveraged its innovative electronic health record to distinguish itself among major employers as a provider of lower-cost care, and even better, as a leader in preventative care. Holston Medical Group uses the clinical data repository and analytics in its EHR to improve treatment of chronic diseases such as diabetes before they become problems, improving patient's lives and dramatically reducing costs for employers.

For example, Eastman Chemical Company—Kingsport's largest employer, with more than 7,000 workers—established a program to pay Holston up to a $250,000 bonus every year that generic drug use rises for its employees. Today, Holston's overall generic rate is an astonishing 82 percent, saving employers such as Eastman millions of dollars each year. Holston Medical Group also has succeeded in reducing worker absenteeism for Eastman, particularly with two strategies that draw upon clinical automation: identifying potential health issues and thus helping to prevent illness, and treating patients efficiently, helping them return to wellness—and work— more quickly.

On a related front, Holston Medical Group has used its electronic health record to enroll thousands of patients in clinical trials, earning a reputation for exceptional speed and efficiency. The National Institutes of Health (NIH) in 2005 named Holston the nation's top enrollment site for the 10,000-patient ACCORD diabetes study, an amazing feat when one considers that the majority of clinical trials are conducted by much larger academic medical centers. Holston attributes its research success to the EHR's ability to quickly and accurately match potential candidates with trial protocols by utilizing the complete health record, including lab test results, prescription drug data, problem lists, and demographics. Moreover, the system greatly reduces the number of patients rejected from each study for failure to meet eligibility requirements or for protocol violations. Overall, the electronic health record has enabled Holston's clinical research program to generate more than $2.5 million in annual revenue—enough to cover research costs, provide significant bonuses to physicians, contribute to the clinic's general overhead, and pay the entire cost of using the EHR for its primary purpose of improving the quality and efficiency of patient care.

As Dr. Miller notes, "It wouldn't be possible for a group our size to earn millions of dollars each year from research without an electronic health record." Still, Dr. Miller is philosophical about automation. "I don't love automation. I went into medical practice to help patients who are sick and to keep them well. But medicine is too complex to provide world-class treatment without world-class tools. I want every physician at Holston to know we've done our best and every patient to understand our commitment."

Conclusion

While I cannot guarantee that every practice that implements an electronic health record will see similar results, I can confidently predict that without it, no practice will be positioned to survive and prosper. That is a reflection of the tremendous change and innovation taking place in healthcare today. From solo family physicians to large academic medical centers, the industry is embracing information technology in order to inform physicians and caregivers at the point of care and connect the system for greater efficiency and quality.

The key to this progress lies in separating myth from reality. We must prove the value of information technology through best demonstrated practices, backed by concrete examples with clear, independent measures of success. As the evidence mounts, more physicians are beginning to acknowledge that healthcare is an information business. They are embracing a future in which clinical automation systems are the standard for delivering world-class care in the most cost-effective manner possible.

Those of us who truly care about healthcare should accept no less.

—⚁—

Glen E. Tullman is Chairman and Chief Executive Officer of Allscripts, the leading provider of clinical software, connectivity, and information services that physicians use to improve healthcare. A magna cum laude graduate of Bucknell University with an advanced degree in Social Anthropology as a Rotary Foundation Fellow at St. Antony's College, Oxford University, Mr. Tullman worked in the Executive Office of the President of the United States under two administrations before entering the business world. Mr. Tullman has run three public companies and is an active venture investor in the healthcare and education sectors. Mr. Tullman, who strongly advocates company and executive-level involvement in charitable and community causes, serves on the board of the Juvenile Diabetes Research Foundation in Chicago and several other public and private boards.

—⚁—

[1] Esther Hing, Donald K. Cherry, and David A. Woodwell "National Ambulatory Medical Care Survey: 2004 Summary," Centers for Disease Control and Prevention. *Advance Data from Vital and Health Statistics,* no. 374 (Hyattsville, MD: National Center for Health Statistics, 2006). Available at http://www.cdc.gov/nchs/data/ad/ad374.pdf (accessed April 6, 2007).

[2] Institute of Medicine, Preventing Medication Errors, July 2006. Available at http://www.iom.edu/Object.File/Master/35/943/medication%20errors%20new.pdf (accessed April 6, 2007).

[3] R. Hillestad et al., "Can Electronic Medical Record Systems Transform Health Care? Potential Health Benefits, Savings and Costs," *Health Affairs* 24, no. 5 (2005): 1103–17.

[4] Stephen L. Badger, Ryan G. Bosch, and Praveen Toteja, "Rapid Implementation of an Electronic Health Record in an Academic Setting," *Journal of Health Information Management* 19, no. 2 (2005): 34–40.

CHAPTER 7

Health Plan Initiatives with Information Technology: Better Knowledge for Healthier Lives

Scott P. Serota

—ɯ—

Editor's Introduction

Cost and quality indicators are heading in the wrong direction, and the need to transform our system grows stronger every day. Health plans are a critical information hub, as they are the key administrators in healthcare and interact with all parties involved. Through these relationships, health plans have helped develop, deploy, and provide incentives for the adoption of health information technology where it matters most—in the physician's office and with consumers. Health plans are working with family physicians, large medical groups, and hospitals of all kinds to better utilize health IT to improve the delivery of care and to make administration more efficient. Health plans have introduced new financing models for consumers, such as high-deductible plans with Health Savings Accounts. They are also deploying personal health records to help consumers learn more about their health and to better understand their healthcare. These initiatives highlight the progress that can—and must—be made when health plans, physicians, hospitals, and consumers use information technology to transform health.

—ɯ—

Recognizing the tremendous potential of health information technology to transform healthcare, health plans across the country are accelerating IT adoption to improve the quality, safety, and efficiency of healthcare in America. Health plans share with the Bush administration, Congress, the Center for Health Transformation, and many others the vision of a nationwide, interoperable health IT infrastructure benefiting all citizens. To become reality, a vision this far-reaching requires collaboration and commitment by all stakeholders—from consumers, employers, and providers to government, health plans, and others.

I am proud to serve as the payer representative on the American Health Information Community, the federally chartered commission convened by Health and Human Services Secretary Michael Leavitt. Our mission is to develop recommendations and obtain cooperation to advance an interoperable nationwide system. In support of this shared vision, our industry is working through public-private partnerships to develop standards for health information exchange, as well as spearheading health IT initiatives in our own communities.

If harnessed effectively, information could fuel great strides to improve healthcare quality, safety, and efficiency. The challenge is getting the right information to the right people—including consumers, physicians, and emergency responders—where and when they need it and in an understandable, usable format. Equally critical, these and other decision-makers need tools to help them translate data and information into knowledge and action so they can make timely, evidence-based healthcare decisions. Health plans connect the healthcare system's many players and are well positioned to collaborate with others to leverage information and help promote widespread adoption of health IT.

A Shared Vision for Health IT

An ideal model of health information technology is for providers to use electronic health records (EHRs) that link to other payers, providers, and consumers. Pertinent health information could thus follow the consumer across the continuum of care and be readily available at the point of service. EHRs would include clinical decision support to ensure that the best diagnostic and treatment information is available to the provider when treating a patient.

An EHR, for example, could alert a doctor that a diabetes patient has not had a recent eye exam, an important standard of care. The ability to link payer administrative data would also enable greater efficiency, allowing doctors and consumers to know instantaneously whether a deductible has been met and what co-payment is required.

In 2005 Hurricane Katrina displaced more than 1 million Gulf Coast residents and destroyed or prevented access to countless paper medical records. This tragedy sharply demonstrated the critical need for electronic records that would quickly communicate health information across state lines. Following the disaster, several Blue Cross and Blue Shield plans in the region accelerated development and rollout of EHRs derived from insurers' claims records, which contained vital health information such as patient health histories, medications, treatment regimens, and test results. This helped maintain continuity of care for many disaster victims who no longer had access to their paper medical records or regular physicians. Although claims-based EHRs are intended to complement, not replace, clinical records, they do begin to address providers' immediate need for better information while electronic medical record systems are under development. With the adoption of national standards, the health IT system of the future will support seamless exchange of both clinical and administrative information.

Clearly, all stakeholders have a role to play in making our shared vision a reality. To effectively advance health IT, we must address and resolve the following issues:

Data Standards

True interoperability requires national, uniform health IT standards that enable all healthcare participants to exchange clinical and administrative information. Addressing the need for standards is an essential first step in building a seamless, nationwide health IT system. All stakeholders must be involved—not only to develop standards, but also to ensure adoption. Public-private partnerships, such as the Health Information Technology Standards Panel, have been created to identify existing standards that support the health IT vision and to determine which additional standards need to be developed.

Collaborative industry initiatives also are helping to identify standards. One such initiative is a joint project of the Blue Cross and Blue Shield Association (BCBSA) and America's Health Insurance Plans (AHIP) to identify standards for electronic personal health records (PHRs). The goal is for PHRs from different health plans and technology vendors to contain a consistent, core set of information, making them easier for consumers and providers to use. BCBSA and AHIP are collaborating with outside experts to develop: (1) a minimum PHR data set based on consumer and provider input, and (2) standards and operating rules to achieve portability, so that a patient's information will transfer from one PHR to another when he or she switches health plans. The data set and standards will be available to the public, so any entity can adopt them. We believe greater continuity will add value to PHRs and help the technology flourish.

Consumer Engagement

The ultimate benefits of health IT belong to consumers—better information will lead to improvements in the safety, quality, and efficiency of care. Consumers are demanding more information about their health and medical care and want it readily available in an understandable, easy-to-use format. Health IT can help meet these consumer requirements, and health plans are delivering these solutions today. As a result, more knowledgeable consumers are being empowered to take greater responsibility for their health and healthcare. They are better-equipped to discuss problems and possible solutions with their providers and to make more educated decisions for themselves and their families. Essentially, better-informed consumers can lead to higher-quality care, healthier lifestyles, and better management of chronic conditions. A healthier population costs less—ultimately helping keep healthcare affordable for all Americans.

Provider Acceptance

Widespread provider adoption is the key to a successful nationwide health IT system. Providers must see the clinical value, the patient benefits, and the business case for adopting health IT. Importantly, new technology must fit into providers' workflow and help increase their efficiency and productivity. Building on extensive, long-standing relationships, the Blues are collaborating closely with providers and provider organizations to help them implement health IT, often in combination with quality improvement initiatives. As providers adopt health IT and pass on its benefits to their patients, healthcare consumers are likely to appreciate its value and seek out providers who use it.

Privacy and Security

Consumers must be assured that their healthcare information remains private, secure, and accurate. Physicians and other stakeholders also must trust in the privacy, security, and accuracy of electronic health information. Strong, uniform protections must be in place, and all entities providing or managing personal health information must follow the HIPAA privacy and security rules.

Until EHRs are widely adopted and a framework of uniform

national data standards to support the wider exchange of clinical information is in place, health plans are the most comprehensive source of health information available. They capture information on the broad range of care based on claims data submitted by many different providers. This includes care for multiple conditions across various providers, settings, and time frames—from doctor visits and hospital admissions to diagnoses, procedures, prescriptions, and other information.

For instance, a family physician may not be aware that she is testing a patient for a condition the patient's cardiologist confirmed two weeks ago, but the patient's health plan has a record of the cardiologist's test and resulting diagnosis. Or a child may arrive at the emergency room for treatment of a puncture wound. His babysitter may not know when he had his last tetanus booster shot, but that information is in his health plan record. The potential to save lives lies also in easy access to pharmacy claims data that can help avoid potentially dangerous drug interactions.

Health Plan Health IT Initiatives: Working Toward the Shared Vision

Across the nation, health plans are collaborating with providers, consumers, and other key stakeholders to promote health IT, tailoring individual initiatives to meet specific community needs. Health plans are:

- Partnering with other stakeholders to enable statewide and regional exchange of health information, in the process creating clinical and administrative interoperability

- Empowering consumers with PHRs, patient-controlled summaries of health information that can be auto-populated by a patient's health plan with claims data, such as medications, diagnoses, and recent healthcare encounters. PHRs also can be self-populated with personal information (e.g., family history and allergies) by the patient

- Creating claims-based EHRs that are embedded with clinical decision support for authorized providers, such as treatment guidelines, screening reminders, and drug interaction alerts

- Helping physicians adopt and use new technologies such as electronic prescribing, which enables providers to automatically transmit prescriptions to the pharmacy and check for drug interactions, proper dosage, and formulary information

- Giving consumers tools to choose the best care by making information on quality and cost readily available

Health IT Partnerships

Throughout the country, health plans are working with state and regional collaborations to promote health information exchanges. These partnerships enable key stakeholders in the community to develop a shared vision and begin laying the groundwork for an interoperable health IT infrastructure.

The Nebraska Health Information Initiative (NeHII), a collaborative effort of the state government, providers, and payers, is building on the state's existing telemedicine network to exchange and analyze health data for the benefit of every Nebraskan. Blue Cross and Blue Shield of Nebraska has helped fund the NeHII planning process with the belief that health IT systems can improve both quality of care and access to care for all Nebraskans. Today, NeHII is in the final stage of determining the types of systems it plans to support across the healthcare community.

In Arkansas, a consortium of providers and payers initiated one of the nation's first statewide interoperable networks providing administrative, financial, and clinical healthcare information to healthcare professionals at the point of service. The Advanced Health Information Network began in 1996 and was built through a partnership of Arkansas Blue Cross and Blue Shield, two of Arkansas's major hospitals, and IBM. This project also gave physicians and hospitals access to electronic medical records and claims databases.

Another example of statewide collaboration is Availity, LLC, a multi-payer electronic data interchange (EDI) connected to 100 percent of hospitals and 94 percent of physician sites in Florida. Availity is a joint venture of Blue Cross and Blue Shield of Florida and Humana, Inc., with participation by a number of other payers in Florida, including Aetna, Inc., CIGNA Corp., and Vista Healthplan, as well as the Florida Hospital Healthcare System. UnitedHealth Group is also participating in a large-scale pilot partnership. The Availity Gateway is a secure, single sign-on portal that allows providers and other healthcare entities to execute real-time information exchange and electronic transactions, such as claims processing and insurance eligibility inquiries. Availity also supports a payer-based EHR.

Personal Health Records

Launched in June of 2005 by Empire Blue Cross and Blue Shield, a subsidiary of WellPoint, Inc., "My Health Record" provides members in New York a robust, consumer-oriented personal health record. Members have online access to their personal medical history and current health profile, based largely on information gleaned from claims and lab results updated automatically by Empire. The content covers medical visits, diagnosed conditions, medications, allergies, surgeries, immunizations, and lab/diagnostic tests and features a medical thesaurus that translates information into lay terminology.

Once registered for My Health Record, members can enter additional details (e.g., family medical history), as well as restrict the display of certain information (such as lab results) for privacy. Members control access to their records by authorizing electronic access for specific providers. These authorizations can be made and tracked online. My Health Record is printable, so patients can take it along on doctor visits and carry it in an emergency wallet card format. My Health Record also assesses users' health risks by linking to self-reported member information submitted through a Health Risk Assessment tool. Patients then receive personalized notices in their online message center about recommended screenings and other important actions to take.

Payer-based Electronic Health Records

Partnering with the state of Tennessee, Blue Cross and Blue Shield of Tennessee broke new ground in 2005 with Shared Health Clinical Health Record™, the nation's largest health information exchange initiative of its kind for a Medicaid population. Shared Health, a wholly owned subsidiary of Blue Cross and Blue Shield of Tennessee, allows registered providers to access a pre-populated electronic record that includes a patient's demographic information, medical diagnoses and procedures, medications, lab results, immunizations, allergies, and vital signs.

In the fall of 2006, Shared Health began offering consumers the opportunity to directly access their Clinical Health Records, providing a link between caregivers and consumers that fosters true empowerment in healthcare. Shared Health projects significant cost savings through improved medication management, reduced clinical waste, and improved compliance with evidence-based medicine guidelines. In July 2006, Shared Health and its partner were awarded one of two contracts by the Centers for Medicare and Medicaid Services to test the feasibility of pre-populating personal health records with Medicare beneficiary claims data.

Electronic Prescribing

Launched in 2003 in order to advance electronic prescribing, the eRx Collaborative consists of Blue Cross and Blue Shield of Massachusetts, Tufts Health Plan, Neighborhood Health Plan, and technology partners ZixCorporation and DrFirst, Inc. The program covers most of the participating physicians' e-prescribing start-up costs, including the sponsorship of handheld devices and software fees for the first year. By supporting e-prescribing for the members of multiple health plans, the program raises its value and convenience for physicians. Onsite training and technical support have also been critical to the program's success. By the end of 2005, 3,400 physicians in the eRx Collaborative submitted 3 million prescriptions electronically. And while the eRx Collaborative helps physicians get started with e-prescribing, Blue Cross and Blue Shield of Massachusetts also offers physician incentives to help expand and sustain the practice, including financial rewards for physicians submitting a target percentage of their prescriptions electronically.

In 2005, the benefits of these e-prescribing initiatives were already apparent:

- In December 2005, physicians and prescribing clinicians in the eRx Collaborative changed more than 5,500 potentially harmful prescriptions as a result of electronic alerts on drug interactions and allergies. In a survey of eRx Collaborative electronic prescribers, 56 percent said e-prescribing improved their ability to work with multiple health plans' formularies, and 47 percent said it saved time for office staff.

- In a November 2005 survey of providers that used eRx Collaborative, more than half said e-prescribing saved time for office staff and 73 percent would recommend the technology to another physician.

- Based on a Blue Cross and Blue Shield of Massachusetts analysis, pharmacy costs among the plan's top electronic prescribers decreased 1.5 percent due to higher utilization of lower-cost preferred brands. Plan members saved, on average, $20 to $25 for each electronic prescription changed in favor of a lower-cost brand—with no decrease in quality.

Healthcare Comparison Tools

Blue Cross and Blue Shield of Minnesota has made it easier for consumers to compare healthcare providers. The Healthcare Facts® online tool provides consumers with straightforward, easy-to-use information for Minnesota hospitals and primary care clinics. Using the familiar "nutrition label" format, it displays objective comparison criteria, including programs/services offered (such as pain management), the number of procedures/cases of a particular type handled annually (such as childbirths and cancer cases), and safety/quality measures (such as the number of inpatients per registered nurse). Healthcare Facts® is available at no cost to consumers via www.healthcarefacts.org and in printed form upon request. General cost comparisons for hospitals are available for all consumers and detailed price information for clinical procedures and visits are accessible to members. The approach enables consumers to make informed, "best fit" decisions about their healthcare providers and choices based on their personal needs and preferences.

Conclusion

In addition to the initiatives highlighted here, health plans have many more health IT projects under way throughout the country. We are gaining valuable experience from these initiatives, which will help us as we work with others toward a nationwide health IT system. Collectively, health plans are committed to building a fully interoperable health IT system that will improve the quality, safety, and efficiency of care. Achieving this goal will take time, and in the interim, the health plan community is being proactive, moving forward with practical, achievable steps to harness healthcare information and spur health IT adoption. These efforts will help us realize our vision of a better healthcare future for America.

—m—

Scott P. Serota is President and CEO of the Blue Cross and Blue Shield Association, a national federation of 39 independent Blue Cross and Blue Shield companies covering more than 98 million Americans. Serota serves on the American Health Information Community, working with HHS to advance health information technology and electronic health records. He also served on the White House Conference on Aging Policy Committee, chairing its Subcommittee on Health.

He is a founding member of the National Business Group on Health's Institute on Healthcare Costs and Solutions, and a board member of the Council for Affordable Quality Healthcare, National Center for Healthcare Leadership, Health Research & Educational Trust, Partnership for Prevention, and Accrediting Commission on Education for Health Services Administration. He is a member of the American College of Healthcare Executives, and serves on the Washington University School of Medicine National Council, chairing the Alumni Association Health Administration Program. He was also named a distinguished alumnus for 2006 by the Purdue College of Science.

CHAPTER 8

Community Health Information Exchanges: The Building Blocks for a Nationwide Health Information Network

Thomas M. Fritz and Jac J. Davies

—ɯ—

Editor's Introduction

Building the health system of tomorrow requires action today, and innovators at the local and regional level are leading the way. Hospitals, physicians, technology vendors, health plans, state and local governments, employers, and consumers are collaborating in hundreds of locations from coast to coast, connecting their communities to improve the delivery and administration of care. The characteristics of these health information exchanges differ greatly from one to the next, just as the communities themselves differ from one to the next—in geographic location, size, scope, sophistication, and stakeholder involvement. Despite these differences, they all face the same challenges in adopting community-wide health information technology, creating a sustainable financial model, protecting patient privacy and confidentiality, and developing true interoperability. The documented successes from pioneering communities—and they are out there—are invaluable as we work toward creating a true nationwide health information network.

—ɯ—

Healthcare is a local phenomenon: referral patterns, relationships, and resources are all critical elements of a healthcare delivery system that occur within a community. Even with strong community referral patterns in place, there can exist real difficulties in sharing the patient information necessary for delivering optimal care. Patient records are captured in multiple facilities, on paper, or in stand-alone electronic medical record systems. When a patient moves from a family doctor to a specialist, or is released back to the family physician's care after a hospital stay, his or her records may or may not follow.

In April 2004, President George W. Bush declared that the majority of Americans should have access to interoperable electronic health records within ten years. To facilitate that vision, he created the Office of the National Coordinator for Health Information Technology (ONCHIT), which was charged with "developing, maintaining, and overseeing a strategic plan to guide nationwide adoption of health information technology in both the public and private sectors."[1] The ONCHIT laid the foundation for that strategic plan in its 2004 report, *The Decade of Health Information Technology*, which specifically calls for the creation of a National Health Information Network (NHIN), defined as "a set of common intercommunication tools such as mobile authentication, Web services architecture, and security technologies."[2]

While the NHIN has become a national goal, community-level networks must be a higher priority because of the need to support health information exchange and improve patient care within local delivery systems. This emphasis at the local level will lead to more effective delivery of care where it is most needed. As local health information exchanges are established, they can be the building blocks for the electronic exchange of health information between communities or across the country. This systematic approach provides the best recipe for a successful nationwide system.

Regional Health Information Organizations

The Decade of Health Information Technology describes one approach to developing community-based health information exchange: through the creation of regional health information organizations (RHIOs). These organizations focus on the secure, electronic exchange of health information among healthcare providers, so patient information is available when and where it is needed. Another term that has been used to describe the RHIO concept is health information exchanges (HIE).

According to the eHealth Initiative, in its *Third Annual Survey of Health Information Exchange at the State, Regional and Community Levels,* there are at least 165 health information exchange initiatives operating in 49 states, the District of Columbia, and Puerto Rico.[3] These initiatives are at varying stages of maturation, with most being in early discussions of governance and structure.

The ultimate goal for RHIOs or HIEs is to develop the infrastructure necessary to securely exchange electronic health information among disparate systems to get the data where it is needed for patient care. Very few organizations have actually reached this goal. One that has is Inland Northwest Health Services (INHS) of Spokane, Washington. INHS provides valuable lessons about creating community collaborations that can result in a sustainable infrastructure to support health information exchange.

Development of a Foundational System

INHS did not set out to be a RHIO. Two competing hospital systems, Providence Services of Eastern Washington (PSEW) and Empire Health Services (EHS), formed INHS in 1994 to provide a neutral organizational home for shared administrative and clinical services that would benefit both systems. The formation of INHS was driven by a common goal—to make previously unprofitable services self-supporting while improving the level of patient care.

Joining forces had the potential to reduce expenses, improve quality, and generate goodwill in the community. The organizational structure of INHS embodies that collaboration. Established as a 501(c)(3), INHS is managed by a board of directors composed of members of the sponsoring hospitals' boards, their respective CEOs, and other medical and community leaders.

As a first step in the collaboration, PSEW and EHS combined their two failing air ambulance services into one joint program that would serve the entire region. Within several years of operation, the joint program, named Northwest MedStar, was operating at a profit. This early effort established a model for equitable treatment across hospital systems and helped to build trust between the organizations.

The next move was to combine low-volume inpatient and outpatient rehabilitation programs into a jointly owned freestanding rehabilitation hospital named St. Luke's Rehabilitation Institute. The resulting consolidation allowed the two hospital systems to turn a history of losses into long-term financial stability.

The following step was considerably more ambitious—to create an integrated hospital information system. As EHS and PSEW were using different information systems, the formation of an integrated system required one of them to completely replace its information technology with that of its competitor. It was a huge leap of faith, but in 1996 PSEW and EHS decided to merge information systems. At the same time, INHS created a new division, Information Resource Management (IRM), to implement and manage the new combined system.

The following year, IRM implemented a common Meditech information system for the six hospitals of EHS and PSEW, which ranged from a 600-bed Spokane hospital to a rural 30-bed facility. The combined information system implemented a single patient identifier, allowing patient records to be electronically accessed between hospitals. PSEW and EHS saw reduced costs for supporting their information systems, as well a decreased proportion of total operating expenses that had to be budgeted for information systems.

Soon, other hospitals in the region were asking to be included in the integrated information system. By 2006, the INHS network had grown to 38 primarily independent hospitals across Washington and Idaho, with an additional four locations soon to be added in southern California. Most of these are small rural hospitals that would not be able to afford advanced health information systems without leveraging their purchasing power through INHS.

Emergence of Health Information Exchange

Shortly after implementing the new systems, area physicians began asking for tools that would make patient data more readily accessible outside the hospital. In 1997, INHS implemented Patient Care Inquiry (PCI), a Meditech tool that allows physicians to view hospital patient information from remote locations. By the end of 2005, more than 800 physicians were regularly using PCI, accessing it more than 60,000 times each month.

The community soon began to recognize that the INHS infrastructure could also serve as the transport system for a variety of other data. In 2002, Inland Imaging, a regional imaging organization, implemented a digital PACS system in its clinics. Rather than building an entirely new network, Inland collaborated with INHS to integrate the PACS data into PCI, allowing physicians to view patients' digital images along with their hospital data. Inland also indexed its system to the INHS Master Patient Index (MPI), ensuring that patient records would be linked across the disparate systems.

In 2004, in order to quickly distribute test results to physicians, INHS worked with Pathology Associates Medical Laboratories (PAML) and its competitor, Quest Diagnostics, to link laboratory results to the Meditech system. This approach reinforced the neutrality of the network. PAML also mapped its patient records to the INHS MPI, leading to a common community-wide process for identifying patients. The result is a robust system that provides physicians with a single source for complete laboratory, imaging, and hospital data, both inpatient and outpatient, from virtually all the facilities in the region.

Spokane is home to a large number of retired and active military personnel. Because they and their families receive care both at military facilities and in the area's civilian hospitals, healthcare providers at Fairchild Air Force Base and the Spokane Veteran's Administration hospital needed access to the information contained in the INHS Meditech system. INHS collaborated with Department of Defense officials to give military clinicians access to Meditech information.

Physician offices in the Spokane area began to acquire electronic health record (EHR) systems in the late 1990s. INHS worked with the various EHR vendors to establish common Health Level Seven (HL7) interfaces to these new systems, which proved to be a major benefit. One internal medicine practice with ten physicians noted that they were able to reduce or redeploy four staff positions due to their new ability to receive patient information electronically, rather than via the hundreds of phone calls or faxes they had typically received each day. In 2006, 33 physician offices representing 576 healthcare providers were routinely receiving HL7 messages from INHS.

INHS was not created in a vacuum. The Spokane area is home to many progressive physicians and other healthcare providers who have embraced information technology in their practices. In 1997, a group of these providers formed the Inland Northwest Community Health Information Project, or INCHIP. The members of INCHIP encouraged adoption of EHRs by physicians' offices in the community and helped to prioritize the various health information technology and information exchange projects being proposed. Its board of directors, which includes representation by physicians, INHS, PAML, and Inland Imaging, helps to assure the integration and coordination of each member's information technology projects.

Leveraging the Foundational System

By 2006, the foundational INHS system had become a platform for a wide variety of initiatives addressing such issues as quality of care, decision support, physician access to information, hospital operations, and public health. INHS has implemented bar-coded medication verification, computerized physician order entry, and tools to provide physicians with wireless access to patient information. INHS has also implemented Web-based tools that help hospital staff monitor the status of the emergency department, patient rooms, and other critical operations.

At the same time that INHS was creating an integrated information system, we began developing an extensive telehealth infrastructure designed to enhance the quality of care delivered to rural patients, called Northwest TeleHealth. The information technology and telehealth infrastructure allow for such innovative programs as TelePharmacy, which lets rural hospitals link to an urban hospital pharmacy in Spokane for oversight of medication administration, and TeleER, which links small rural emergency departments with a Level Two trauma facility for consultation. Both programs rely on videoconferencing to connect the healthcare providers and the information system to share patient data. Because of these programs, patients at these facilities receive higher-quality care; they would otherwise have no access to specialized or expert opinion and guidance.

While the primary focus of all the INHS initiatives is clinical care, the integrated information system also provides a valuable source of data to inform and support public health actions. De-identified data has been used by public health agencies to assess particular health outcomes and to support emerging syndromic surveillance systems. Identified data is reported electronically to public health agencies when required under state regulations.

Privacy and Security

All clinical information systems operated by INHS have been designed to protect the privacy and security of patients' personal health information. While the Meditech system for hospitals and the EHR systems for physicians' offices are physically managed as a single database, the databases are virtually segregated so that individuals within any participating healthcare facility have access only to data on that particular facility's patients. All access is role-based, so staff can see only the information they need in order to carry out their job. Each facility maintains its own privacy policies and also agrees to abide by privacy policies established by INHS for its network members.

For a physician to access patient information from the Meditech system, he or she must be identified as that patient's provider of record. Providers of record also have the ability to grant access to other physicians for referrals or specialist care. Emergency room personnel can access patient information without prior permission from the primary care provider.

All access to patient data is governed by HIPAA and state privacy laws. The standard paperwork signed by patients during the admission process grants the healthcare organization the ability to share the patient's data as necessary to support the delivery of care.

Funding

The region's health information exchange infrastructure has been developed with no federal or state grants or loans. These achievements were possible because members of the Spokane healthcare community were willing and able to leverage their existing resources and to make smart purchasing and implementation decisions. When planning and purchasing new IT systems, healthcare organizations have learned to consider the information technology decisions made by others in the community. This collaborative approach has allowed all members of the region's healthcare system to maximize their existing information management dollars.

Looking Ahead

INHS is continuing to expand health information exchange in the Spokane community and around the region and to replicate the model in communities outside the region. Future plans include sharing data with pharmacies and nursing homes, implementing personal health records, and enabling efficient movement of data among physicians' offices. In a first step toward bi-directional electronic information exchange, INHS has initiated a project with the Community Health Association of Spokane (CHAS), a network of federally qualified health clinics, to routinely move data from the CHAS EHR to the INHS system. This will allow physicians who see CHAS patients in the emergency room to have access to those patients' clinical records.

An important requirement for the success of a comprehensive health information exchange will be the wholesale adoption of EHRs by physicians throughout the region. To make it easier for physicians to acquire and operate EHRs, INHS established a physician EHR service in 2004. This program is based on an Application Services Provider (ASP) model, with INHS hosting the EHR software on central servers and making the software available to physicians over the organization's network. The ASP approach reduces the EHR start-up costs and simplifies its operation for physicians. In addition, it has enabled INHS to automatically populate the EHRs with data from the Meditech system. A total of 38 clinics with 250 providers were utilizing the ASP EHR systems in 2006.

As INHS has grown and developed new approaches to leveraging health information technology, so has the partnership that began with the Inland Northwest Community Health Information Project. Recognizing the need for more formal governance, in 2005 INCHIP agreed to transition into the Northwest Regional Health Information Organization. This body will make decisions on health information technology funding for the entire community, helping to create a greater role for consumers in planning and decision-making and to create educational information about the health information exchange for patients, physicians, and the public.

Lessons Learned

In its 12-year history, INHS has learned how to make collaborative efforts successful while avoiding pitfalls. The following are some examples of knowledge that has contributed to the organization's and the community's success at leveraging health information technology to improve the delivery and quality of healthcare.

Build the business case

Without a demonstrated business case, a collaborative or shared-services organization will not survive past the initial seed funding. The business case should be clearly laid out in the first stage. This early definition may not capture all the goals of participating organizations, but it should identify enough realistic benefits to encourage participants to support the cause.

Start small and grow

Regardless of size, successful businesses and health information exchanges tend to start small. Trying to accomplish too much from the beginning virtually assures complexity, delay, disillusionment, and failure. The initial scope should be realistic and achievable while allowing room for growth.

Demonstrate success

While members of a collaboration generally recognize that it can take time to return real benefit, support will quickly wane if some successes cannot be demonstrated in the short term. Designing a health information exchange initiative with some early successes in mind will increase the likelihood of its survival.

Leverage existing resources and purchasing power

Many of the emerging RHIOs around the country are either hoping for or relying on grant funding before they begin any real activity. Long-term success requires local investment, not government hand-outs. All healthcare organizations spend money every day to manage health information. Creatively redirecting those funds and collaborating on purchases with other healthcare organizations can provide the funds necessary for health information exchange initiatives.

Standardize

Standardization saves money throughout the healthcare system and improves quality of care. Standardized technology allows for joint purchases that reduce cost and shared services to support maintenance and operation. Standardized data systems allow electronic information exchange and less likelihood of error when comparing data from different sources.

Maintain neutrality

Because the healthcare environment is usually highly competitive, health information exchange initiatives may not succeed due to perceived or real bias. Collaborations or shared services organizations must establish and actively support a neutral stance in their dealings with all community partners.

Recognize that community governance organizations take work

The convening organization must keep reminding participants why they are working together and provide them a safe environment for doing so. The participants must be encouraged to put aside differences in order to work for the community good and to recognize that people and organizations will occasionally leave the table, in spite of the group's best efforts. Successful community organizations are the ones ready to welcome them back.

—∿—

Thomas M. Fritz, M.A., M.P.A., has more than 25 years of experience in private and government-run hospital and healthcare delivery systems. He is currently CEO of Inland Northwest Health Services (INHS) in Spokane, Washington, a hospital-based not-for-profit joint venture between two competing integrated healthcare delivery systems. INHS provides a variety of services, including a freestanding physical medicine and rehabilitation hospital, the region's air ambulance system, a community health education program, a regional telehealth network, and an integrated hospital information system that currently supports 38 hospitals in three states. Mr. Fritz is also a member of the Board of Trustees for the Certification Commission for Healthcare Information Technology. In the past, Mr. Fritz has served as a representative to the Joint Commission for the Accreditation of Healthcare Organizations (JCAHO), as the CEO of Eastern State Hospital in Washington State, and as the State Director for Alcoholism, Drug Abuse, and Mental Health in Delaware.

Jac J. Davies, M.S., M.P.H., is the Director of Program Development for Inland Northwest Health Services. Ms. Davies is responsible for identifying new opportunities for program growth and new partnerships for INHS. She also oversees a continuing education program for health professionals in rural communities. In addition, Ms. Davies facilitates planning activities for area healthcare organizations interested in health information exchange. Prior to joining INHS, Ms. Davies worked at the Washington State Department of Health, where she served as Assistant Secretary for the Division of Epidemiology, Health Statistics and Public Health Laboratories. Ms. Davies sits on the boards of the Foundation for Health Care Quality and the Washington State Public Health Association, and she is a clinical faculty member of the Center for Public Health Informatics at the University of Washington. She has an M.S. and an M.P.H. from the University of Washington and a B.S. from the Mississippi University for Women.

—ɯ—

[1] Department of Health and Human Services, *The Decade of Health Information Technology: Delivering Consumer-Centric and Information-Rich HealthCare,* July 21, 2004. Available at http://www.hhs.gov/healthit/documents/hitframework.pdf (accessed April 6, 2007).

[2] Ibid.

[3] eHealth Initiative, *Improving the Quality of Healthcare through Health Information Exchange: Selected Findings from eHealth Initiative's Third Annual Survey of Health Information Exchange at the State, Regional and Community Levels,* September 26, 2006. Available at http://toolkits.ehealthinitiative.org/assets/Documents/eHI2006HIESurveyReportFinal09.25.06.pdf (accessed April 6, 2007).

CHAPTER 9

State Government Initiatives:
Convener, Partner, and Leader in Developing
Statewide Health Information Networks

Mark E. Frisse, M.D. and W. Michael Heekin

—⚶—

Editor's Introduction

Health information technology is a top priority for the private sector and policymakers in Washington, D.C., but hundreds of initiatives at the state and local levels have given the issue even more momentum. The federal government and all fifty states are moving in the right direction, with governors, state legislatures, and local leaders working to make health IT an integral part of transforming health and healthcare. And they are well positioned to do so. In addition to being health insurers and regulators that can drive health IT, state governments have changed the way they purchase healthcare to promote the adoption of interoperable IT, and they have convened and coordinated many local and regional connectivity networks. Many of these initiatives have engaged all the key stakeholders who deliver and administer care to patients, which complements the policy work at the national level. A national plan that builds on the strengths of federal, state, and local leaders will forge a more productive collaboration—and the American people will reap the benefits.

—⚶—

In 2004, President George W. Bush set the goal of delivering an electronic health record to every American and establishing an integrated nationwide health information network by the year 2014. We are behind schedule. There has been noteworthy progress by some organizations, but the endeavor needs to be accelerated. The surest way to succeed is to build a strong, collaborative, and equitable partnership among local, state, and national interests in which each partner plays a distinct yet complementary role.

The need for an effective health information infrastructure is compelling. The ability of our healthcare system to address disease prevention and treatment has not kept pace with the growing challenges of our aging population and complexity of healthcare delivery and financing. If individuals are to receive the information and care they need to improve their own health, having patient data at the point of care through a coordinated health information infrastructure is essential.

To accomplish this and to meet the ambitious goals laid out by President Bush and others, we must navigate a series of unprecedented challenges. They include:

- Convening and engaging a diverse group of healthcare stakeholders, including doctors, hospitals, health plans, employers, consumers, public health officials, and other government agencies—some of which have distrusted each other and have been reluctant to collaborate as partners

- Establishing a working consensus on the need for a health information network and a shared vision of the structure and benefits to be derived from it

- Motivating healthcare stakeholders to share health information—which can often be contrary to prudent business practices—in pursuit of a higher purpose

- Providing consumers with information on healthcare cost and quality so they can make informed decisions

- Focusing provider attention more on delivering healthcare and less on navigating complex administrative issues

- Convincing investors to commit their resources to develop expensive, somewhat unproven information architecture and technologies without an established business case

- Persuading skeptical stakeholders, including consumers, legislators, and regulators, that perceived risks to privacy and data security posed by an integrated health information network are outweighed by its potential benefits

- Navigating the difficult process of reforming statutes on privacy, health information, and medical malpractice

- Persuading and educating stakeholders to adopt and use the network

- Navigating all these challenges against considerable bureaucratic headwinds at both the national and state levels

Many of these factors have caused the nationwide health information network initiative to lag behind the pace necessary to meet the president's 2014 goal.[1] One key reason for this is that, in our opinion, action must be focused on the local level, rather than a top-down, heavily federal approach dictating the process.[2] Due to the local nature of healthcare delivery, where federal pronouncements often amount to unfunded mandates, the federal top-down approach is difficult to pull off and will likely not lead to success.

A more effective way is to begin with individuals in a constructive, bottom-up collaboration among local, state, and federal stakeholders. Local initiatives are at the forefront of the health information connectivity movement. They, along with state and national partners, must play distinct and critical roles in an integrated effort. Initiatives outside Washington have exceeded the modest progress made at the national level, and these should be the focal point for federal action. More than 200 local health information exchanges[3] and at least 38 state-level initiatives are in planning or implementation stages with limited federal involvement.[4]

Below is a brief description of the roles that the local, state, and national tiers of the integrated initiative must assume in order to be successful.

Role of the Local Network Organization

Like politics, healthcare is, for the most part, local. Many communities—both large and small—have begun working toward connectivity within local geographic areas, be they intrastate or interstate. These local networks should form the basic building blocks of the nationwide health information network. In keeping with its role on the front lines, the local organization serves many functions that are critical to the success of the local/state/national "ecosystem," including:

- Establishing and maintaining working relationships among providers, consumers, employers, and all healthcare stakeholders who will support the network. It is easier to maintain a constructive dialogue among employers, providers, and other stakeholders at the local level with organizations and entities they know and trust

- Addressing information security and confidentiality concerns. Most information practices required to gain the public trust are not governed by HIPAA but by higher standards maintained by healthcare providers and other parties within the locality or state.

- Setting priorities for the goals of the health information network, such as the coordination of care, quality metrics, public health functionalities, health plan reimbursement reforms (e.g., pay for performance), and so on. The local network organization is best suited to identify and set these priorities, as it is responsible for delivering better quality care to patients. Accurate and complete information at the point of care will facilitate this.

- Establishing the business model of the health information network, including the portfolio of products and services to be delivered

- Promoting adoption and utilization of the network by marketing network services and enrolling and training healthcare providers and other network customers

The leadership of local organizations will do well enough just to clear the hurdles outlined above. They should strongly consider outsourcing tasks that do not lie directly on the critical path to success. Among the functions that might be properly outsourced are the operation of the network's infrastructure, technical support, revenue cycle management, marketing, and enrollment and training of authorized users.

Ideally, the local network organizations within the state and the state-level organization should consider jointly developing or procuring infrastructure and other technical services for the entire statewide network in order to create positive economies of scale. By the same logic, local organizations should not set network standards.

This is a clear example of how the federal efforts, like the Health Information Technology Standards Panel, have been effective—and vital.

Role of the State Network Organization

There is little overlap between what a local initiative must do to succeed and what the national effort must do, with one exception: they must both coordinate their activities with the state organization.

The state-level initiative plays a central role, and for good reason. State organizations are uniquely positioned to promote the success of the health information network within the state. States must deal with the special needs of their population: they bear the brunt of care across the continuum, including care for the uninsured, the elderly, the young, the infirm, and the undocumented; they administer Medicaid, the most complex healthcare program in the country; and they can create incentives for enhancing the quality of care and financing new facilities. Most significant, regarding health information technology, some states have already shown a readiness to commit resources and to develop a coordinated statewide health information infrastructure.[5]

With these considerations in mind, statewide organizations, led by the state government as senior partner, should perform the following functions:

- Convene state-level leaders from all healthcare stakeholders and promote an environment for collaboration and constructive action. Examples of instances in which state government could be helpful as convener or advocate include:

  - Intervening with federal agencies, especially the Centers for Medicare & Medicaid Services (CMS), on behalf of the state and/or local initiatives

  - Intervening with its own bureaucracy on such matters as obtaining access to critical patient data held by state agencies such as Medicaid and the public health department

  - Obtaining statewide network access to patient information

held by health plans, national healthcare companies (e.g., laboratories and pharmacies), and other private data sources

- Invest in network infrastructure development and startup costs. As anyone involved in a health information network initiative is acutely aware, there is a "chicken and egg" dynamic in financing: it is hard to attract investors until the network proves itself successful, and it is hard to prove the network successful until investors provide resources. The state government is uniquely positioned to invest risk capital in the initiative, in light of the significant potential benefits to the state and its citizens when the network proves effective.

- Commit at an early date to purchase network services. Medicaid, the state health department, the state emergency management agency, the division of state employee group insurance, and other state agencies are potential customers of a state's health information infrastructure. The state's leadership in committing to purchase network services will be critical to the early success of the health information network and will make it easier for the network to convince other potential customers to participate.

- Reform state laws and regulations to conform to the realities of electronic health information. The state government is likely to be the final arbiter of questions regarding privacy, data ownership, tort liability, and other legal issues critical to the network's ultimate success. In every jurisdiction that implements and operates a health information network, there should be a wholesale review of state law and statutes, and regulations will almost certainly need to be revised and updated.

- Designate, adopt, and enforce network data standards. Nationally or federally specified standards must be followed so that local communities and statewide efforts are interoperable.

- Promote the effectiveness and sustainability of the local networks in a state or region. In performing that duty, the state organization, in partnership with its constituent local groups and with their agreement, should:

- Facilitate meetings among the local organizations to exchange ideas and lessons learned in order to reduce the duplication of effort and to promote knowledge transfer

- Negotiate group purchasing agreements with vendors on behalf of local networks

- Negotiate revenue opportunities on a statewide scale to be shared with local networks (e.g., clinical trial recruitment contracts)

- Facilitate funding of local networks, even if the state organization itself does not provide the source of funding

- Provide connectivity between local networks and the nationwide infrastructure and maintain a network interface between local, statewide, and nationwide data sources

- Possibly provide local organizations with common network and administrative services, upon mutual agreement

- Provide local network-type services and related assistance to areas within the state, such as rural areas, that are not adequately served by local network initiatives

Developing a High-performance State-level Initiative

State-level organizations are hard at work today in the roles listed above. They are collaborating with local organizations to implement statewide health information infrastructures across the country. And there are many lessons to be learned.

The State Initiative's Charter and Structure
The first step of any statewide effort is to establish a charter document that explicitly describes the organization of the initiative, the respective roles of all participants, the mission, and the desired outcomes. A charter document can be an executive order, state statute, or administrative rule. Although non-governmental charters are a possible option, because the state is an indispensable party to the state-level initiative, a state charter makes for a stronger relationship.

Second, strong consideration should be given to including an advisory board that is broadly representative of all healthcare stakeholders in the state. The initiative must operate with transparency and inclusiveness, and appointing a broadly based advisory board is the first opportunity to demonstrate that principle.

Third, the advisory board should frame broad strategic direction and general oversight of the early phases of the initiative. By doing this, the strategic vision will represent the healthcare stakeholders in the state. Further, the initiative critically needs creativity, imagination, and energy—all commodities the board members can supply in the early stages.

Fourth, to the extent possible, the state's political and policy leaders should avoid the temptation to couple the health information network project with ancillary issues. For example, some jurisdictions have tasked their health information network initiative with responsibility for handling transparency, safety, quality, pay-for-performance, genetic testing, and other projects.[6] While those policy initiatives have merit and address pressing problems facing American healthcare, many have entrenched opponents and deep-rooted supporters. The political energy generated by the depth of those convictions unfortunately can spill over into the health information network undertaking, unnecessarily generating political opposition for the network simply because it is "in the line of fire." Combining those tangential issues also dilutes resources and attention from the already difficult, resource-starved mission of establishing a state health information network.

Finally, the advisory board and the implementing state government structure should be chartered for a limited period of time, such as three to five years, to stress the urgency of developing the state's health information network.

Gubernatorial Leadership

The political leadership should consider housing the initiative within the office of the governor, or an equivalent situation "close to the flagpole," to promote regular and effective access to the state's executive leadership. Statewide initiatives will gain credibility and strength with the governor as an executive sponsor. Also, the only "compensation" that volunteer board members receive is the occasional direct contact with the state's political leaders to brief them firsthand on the progress of the initiative. This contact between the board and political leaders will keep the board members moving ahead and will ensure that state leaders stay in touch with the vision and energy of the initiative. These briefings should occur on a regular basis, even if only twice a year.

Relations with State Bureaucracy

It is important to foster a close working relationship with state government agencies that deal directly with health issues. This can be done by inviting and encouraging staff from relevant agencies to provide guidance and leadership. Government staff members are highly knowledgeable and have the greatest understanding of the issues, especially the political ones, and are generally highly motivated to work for the initiative's success.

Getting Started

With those considerations as the starting point in the framework for relations with the state bureaucracy, the initiative should be seen for what it is: a large-scale transformation similar to efforts that have taken place in business and government.[7] Those involved in this transformation should consider the following steps:

- Create a guiding coalition around the general vision of a statewide network involving as many executive and legislative leaders as possible. Securing a small group of advocates at the top of government is necessary, but it is not sufficient to pull the initiative through the inevitable bureaucratic challenges. In a political coalition, there is strength in numbers. Coalition members may focus on the direct financial benefits of a more effective healthcare delivery system, and/or the broader, long-term social and economic advantages of healthier communities.

- Employ sound project management principles, including guidance by a strategic plan prepared by and/or approved by the advisory board, with specific milestones and metrics of success

- Communicate the vision, strategic plan, and operational milestones to the appropriate constituencies within the state government (and beyond) to promote understanding of and support for the initiative. A lack of understanding leads most to assume the worst, and this clearly does not promote full and enthusiastic cooperation by state government leadership.

- Set appropriate expectations. Unpleasant surprises can be unsettling and sometimes career-ending for even the most dedicated civil servants.

- Engage and mobilize the energies and resources of a broad community of stakeholders. Broad consensus, like state executive leadership buy-in, can help pull the initiative through some hard times.

These steps do not ensure success, but they do ensure a chance at success.

Role of the Nationwide Network Organization

Moving beyond local communities and statewide efforts, there is a developing consensus that the nationwide health information network will comprise a "network of networks." This makes building solid and successful networks at the state and local levels all the more imperative, as a weak foundation cannot support an effective nationwide network.

The role of national leaders at the top of the pyramid is equally critical. The nationwide network organization, while removed from the actual delivery of care, is at the epicenter of national policymaking, federal funding sources, and federal programs. It should be counted upon to perform the following vital functions:

- Establishing and executing a plan for developing and financing an integrated nationwide health information network. This and developing data standards of interoperability are the most critical actions the federal leadership can make. This plan must embrace and build on what is happening today in localities, states, and regions across the country, and it must include specific milestones to hit and clear metrics of success. The Strategic Framework published in 2004 by the Office of the National Coordinator for Health Information Technology was effective at framing the challenge. Federal officials must now delve deeper into the details by integrating existing local and state connectivity efforts into the nationwide plan and outlining specific strategies and measures of success.

- Revisiting the basic questions that are critical to success:

  - What is the vision of the nationwide health information network? What do we want our system to do when it is built? We may want to add more features once the base network is built, but at a minimum, what do we want "Version 1.0" to do?

  - What are the most appropriate and effective roles of local, state, and federal leaders? What are the roles of health plans, providers, and other stakeholders?

  - What is the long-term financing plan? Who will pay for what? How can we ensure financial sustainability?

  - Are there models of successful national initiatives in the past that could guide our approach to accomplishing this complex and important initiative, such as the interstate highway system, the prosecution of World War II, the Marshall Plan, and landing on the moon?

- Convening local, state, federal, and other vital partners, such as Medicare, Medicaid, national health plans, employers, pharmacies, and information technology community, to promote collaborative effort on infrastructure, business model development, public policy, federal funding, and advocacy. The planning process described above will provide an early opportunity to constructively convene these parties. Using the American Health Information Community structure as a starting point, the federal initiative could convene a more broadly inclusive group of stakeholders, particularly state and local leaders, to focus solely on issues directly related to the health information network.

- Modernizing Medicare, as an insurer and trendsetter, to promote the viability and effectiveness of a nationwide health information network, and obtaining equivalent actions from other federal agencies

- Developing and enforcing network data standards of interoperability

- Overseeing the operation of the entire nationwide network

By playing these roles, national leaders have the potential to quickly develop a productive approach to building an interoperable nationwide network. But this starts with integrating state and local leaders into the federal efforts. An equitable and coordinated collaboration between local, state, and federal plans is a winning solution in reaching our shared goals.

Conclusion

After three years of working toward the 2014 goal articulated by President Bush, it is clear that federal, state, and local leaders need to forge a more constructive and collaborative partnership.

Each partner has essential and complementary roles to play. The local communities convene, motivate, and mobilize stakeholders; develop and deliver marketable products and network services to improve patient care; govern the operations of their networks; and act as front-line guardians against misuses of data.

The state and federal partners convene associations of stakeholders to develop network technical paradigms, helpful legislation, and buy-in from critical agencies in the government bureaucracy. State and federal partners also leverage their status as large health plans, healthcare purchasers, employers, regulators, and legislators to develop the business case for an integrated nationwide network. The roles of the national and state partners differ in that the federal level must lead preparation and execution of the overall plan for the integrated nationwide health information network, including data standards of interoperability. On the other hand, state initiatives should be responsible for promoting the effectiveness and viability of local networks.

Ideally, federal, state, and local organizations will embrace these complementary roles to collaborate in a spirit of partnership. There are good reasons why they should work together on this important undertaking, and no good reasons why they should not. In the absence of a constructive relationship, state-level initiatives should continue to work with their constituent local organizations to implement statewide network solutions. They should then collaborate with their state-level counterparts in other jurisdictions.

One way or another, we will build a nationwide health information network that modernizes the delivery and administration of care. The American people are demanding it, and they deserve nothing less.

—⚚—

Mark E. Frisse, M.D., M.B.A., serves as Director of Regional Informatics Programs through the Vanderbilt Center for Better Health and as Professor in the Vanderbilt Department of Biomedical Informatics. In his work at the Vanderbilt Center for Better Health, he is responsible for coordinating regional, state, and national projects aimed at the application of information technology to advance patient care. His primary focus is on developing a state-wide health information infrastructure to support TennCare patients and on developing a regional demonstration in the Memphis area. Prior to assuming his position at Vanderbilt, Dr. Frisse was with First Consulting Group's Clinical Transformation Practice, and prior to this position, he was Chief Medical Officer and Vice President, Clinical Information Services at Express Scripts. Dr. Frisse received his M.D. and M.B.A. from Washington University and received a master's degree in Medical Computer Science from Stanford University. He was a member of the National Research Council's Committee on Enhancing the Internet for Health Applications and more recently was an author of a national report on ePrescribing prepared by the eHealth Initiative.

W. Michael Heekin, J.D., M.B.A., chairs the Florida Governor's Health Information Infrastructure Advisory Board. He was a founding board member and the first chief operating officer of WebMD. Earlier in his career, among other things, Mr. Heekin was an officer on active duty in the U.S. Army and an associate dean at the Florida State University College of Law. Mr. Heekin serves on the Executive Board of the Boy Scouts' Atlanta Area Council, the Executive Advisory Board of the H. Lee Moffitt Cancer Center Total Cancer Care initiative, and the Board of Trustees of the University of Florida Law Center Association. He earned a Master of Business Administration at the Wharton School of the University of Pennsylvania, and law and accounting degrees from the University of Florida.

—⚚—

[1] General Accounting Office, *HHS Is Taking Steps to Develop a National Strategy,* May 2005. Available at http://www.gao.gov/new.items/d05628.pdf (accessed April 6, 2007).

[2] The recently initiated State Alliance for e-Health to be performed under a federal contract by the NGA Center for Best Practices is an example of the "top-down" approach.

[3] Foundation of Research and Education, American Health Information Management Association, *Final Report on Development of State-Level HIE Initiatives,* September 2006. Available at http://www.staterhio.org/documents/Final_Report_HHSP23320064105EC_090106_000.pdf (accessed April 6, 2007).

[4] eHealth Initiative, *Improving the Quality of Healthcare through Health Information Exchange: Selected Findings from eHealth Initiative's Third Annual Survey of Health Information Exchange at the State, Regional and Community Levels,* September 26, 2006. Available at http://toolkits.ehealthinitiative.org/assets/Documents/eHI2006HIESurveyReportFinal09.25.06.pdf (accessed April 6, 2007).

[5] See, for example, HEAL NY. Available at http://www.health.state.ny.us/funding/rfa/0604261035/0604261035.pdf (accessed March 23, 2007).

[6] The federal organization is susceptible to the same political dynamic, as is unfortunately demonstrated in the multitude of ancillary issues currently under study by the Office of National Coordinator for Health Information Technology and the American Health Information Community. See, for example, http://www.hhs.gov/healthit/ahic/index.html.

[7] J. P. Kotter, "Why Transformation Efforts Fail," *Harvard Business Review,* March–April 1995: 59-67.

CHAPTER 10

Advancing Research and Clinical Improvement through Health Information Technology: The Power of Aggregated Data

Beryl L. Vallejo, Dr.P.H., R.N., Richard Bankowitz, M.D., M.B.A., F.A.C.P.
Meg Horgan, R.N., M.S.N. and Eugene A. Kroch, Ph.D.

—ɯ—

Editor's Introduction

When medical data is turned into secure, actionable knowledge, money—and lives—are saved. Data can identify the sickest patients who need the most help, patients genetically predisposed for specific diseases, the best and worst doctors, treatments that work and those that do not, and other vital information. But today's healthcare system is not designed to deliver this kind of knowledge. Data is largely confined to paper medical records scattered across the spectrum of care, with virtually no way to aggregate it from all the disparate sources. As physicians, hospitals, and health plans embrace health information technology and begin to collect and securely share electronic data, we will have the ability to gain invaluable insights into community health, effective treatment regimens, compliance with clinical guidelines, and physician performance. By balancing aggregate data collection and analytics with iron-clad privacy protections, we can deliver the knowledge needed to improve the health of millions of citizens, transforming healthcare in America.

—ɯ—

The Institute of Medicine (IOM) defines quality as the "degree to which health services for individuals and populations increase the likelihood of desired health outcomes and are consistent with current professional knowledge."[1] The IOM has provided a broad framework for defining and evaluating healthcare quality across six attributes: high-quality care is that which is safe, effective, efficient, patient-centered, equitable, and accessible.

Avedis Donabedian developed a healthcare quality measurement system centered on a structure-process-outcomes triad.[2] In the

Donabedian model, *structural quality* refers to health system capabilities, such as credentials of the doctors and nurses, characteristics of the building, etc., while *process quality* assesses interactions among patients and providers. Good process measures are supported by scientific evidence linking them to improved health outcomes. For example, processes that support early and appropriate antibiotic therapy result in decreased mortality for patients with community-acquired pneumonia. Similarly, the best outcome measures are strongly related to process measures that are influenced through the healthcare system. Outcome measures can be short-term (development of complications during a particular hospitalization; response to intravenous pain medication) or long-term (HbA1c values and the development of diabetes retinopathy and blindness; mortality rates after treatment for early stage breast cancer treatment, etc.). All three dimensions (structure, process, and outcomes) provide valuable information for measuring quality and for providing an evidence base for healthcare interventions.

Evidence-based medicine entails integrating individual clinical expertise with the best available clinical evidence from systematic research.[3] The objective is for patients to receive high-quality, effective care that is supported by scientific research. Unfortunately, variability in actual clinical practice is rampant and experts estimate that up to 55 percent of Americans do not receive even the most basic evidence-based care.[4] While this number is breathtaking by itself, it does not begin to address the even more startling issue that the vast majority of medical care is not based on any evidence or driven by data at all. Several studies conclude that as little as 10 percent of all care is actually driven by scientific research—the rest is merely opinion.[5] The collection and analysis of aggregated clinical data can change this.

New organizational structures and initiatives may help to accelerate improvements in healthcare quality and the adoption of evidence-based practices. The Centers for Medicare and Medicaid Services (CMS), Agency for Healthcare Research and Quality (AHRQ), Joint Commission for the Accreditation of Healthcare Organizations (JCAHO), and National Committee for Quality Assurance (NCQA)—along with researchers, payers, and professional organizations—have developed measurement systems to compare and contrast healthcare providers and institutions. At the heart of this effort is the widespread aggregation and dissemination of data.

Measuring Quality through Aggregated Data

Although the debate about how to measure inpatient (hospital) quality of care has often focused on different aspects of Donabedian's 1966 structure-process-outcomes triad, the spotlight on observable outcomes has brought current approaches to hospital quality into line with the ideas of Joseph Juran, which define manufacturing quality as the absence of defects.[6] Under this construct, counting deaths, complications, unusually long hospital stays, unscheduled ICU admissions, and other sentinel events that are deemed universally negative (or nearly so) would signal how much a care provider departs from "good quality."

The availability of structured data collected from a wide variety of institutions makes it possible to construct and model such outcomes. Data on aggregate performance is already being collected, such as HEDIS® data from health plans and Joint Commission Core Measure data from hospitals. Fundamentally, anonymous patient-level data could be collected from each encounter, as is currently being done with MEDPAR, which is discharge abstract data on patients covered by Medicare. This data, when aggregated within the model framework, provides meaningful performance measures that can be evaluated along the IOM's six components of high-quality care.

Evaluation of outcomes often requires comparison among providers. To be meaningful, such comparisons must take into account differences in patient characteristics, severity of illness, and other similar factors, so that a hospital's and/or physician's outcome rates can be compared to the expected rates (or outcome risks) suggested by the underlying patient population. Expected outcome rates for any facility or group of patients are based on the characteristics of those patients applied to a model of the relationship between patient characteristics and outcomes. The population can be restricted to a single provider or a health system over a limited period of time or can encompass a broad range of providers across the country over several years. The more encompassing the population, the broader the basis for comparison.

One favored variant is to calibrate a model of hospitalization outcomes and related performance measures on a nationally based sample of discharges.[7] The aim is to construct a set of parameter estimates for each outcome measure that can be used to predict outcome rates for any set of patients. Six common outcomes include in-hospital mortality, major complication-related morbidity, complication frequency, length of stay, charges, and costs.[8] Predicted rates for these outcomes can be compared to the actual rates to evaluate performance for any set of patients—of a particular facility, service line, diagnosis, age grouping, or treating/attending physician.

This approach has a number of advantages over the alternative method of separately calibrating the risk model on each individual provider, hospital, or hospital system. First, outcome risks that are derived from nationally estimated weights can be compared across all facilities and all physicians, no matter where they practice. Second, any set of discharges can be analyzed, no matter how small, as the model parameters themselves do not need to be estimated from the analysis data set. Third, having a predetermined set of risk parameters allows for real-time evaluation of patient care.

Measuring Dimensions of Performance

When data from many providers is available in a structured format, overall provider performance can be tracked along separate, potentially related dimensions. In the CareScience™ rating model, working with patient-level data from public sources and private subscribers,[9] performance is tracked along two dimensions: clinical quality and efficiency. Clinical quality is measured by the risk-adjusted rate of adverse outcomes (mortality, morbidity, and complications) combined in an empirically derived consumer preference ordering.[10] Efficiency is captured by length of stay and cost.* Within each disease grouping, hospitals are ranked for clinical quality and efficiency separately. The highest rankings within each disease grouping or service line go to hospitals with the lowest risk-adjusted LOS (cost) and adverse outcome rates. This rating system is disease-specific and not explicitly a hospital-level ranking system.

To be singled out as exemplary performers for a given disease, a facility must be in the top two quintiles for both efficiency and clinical quality. Because this rating system is two-dimensional, it does not explicitly trade off clinical quality and efficiency. The five-by-five

---

* Cost comparisons across providers, especially hospitals, can be fraught with arbitrary differences in accounting conventions among operating units, leaving length of stay as a more reliable and comparable proxy for resource usage.

efficiency/quality matrix is illustrated in Figure One. Because the rankings are only weakly correlated in practice (i.e., they are fairly evenly distributed across the grid), exemplary performance ("High") facilities constitute 16 percent (40 percent of 40 percent) of all that qualify for ranking. At the other end of the spectrum are the bottom two quintiles for both efficiency and quality (four poor performance "Low" cells). Three other designations cover the middle ranges: the average performance of the "Middle" five cells, six low-quality, high-efficiency cells, and the opposing six high-quality, low-efficiency cells. The objective for any provider is to move toward the "northeast."

In this context, high-quality and high-efficiency ("Select Practice") hospitals are those where patients are least likely to suffer adverse outcomes and where care is delivered without squandering scarce resources. These are hospitals with the lowest rates of preventable deaths and debilitating complications of care. Their lengths of stay are no longer than necessary to ensure the best possible outcomes.

In identifying these hospitals (and their opposites in the quality-efficiency spectrum), no attempt is made to second-guess their care processes and protocols, as is done when CMS and the Joint Commission monitor so-called appropriate care ("core") measures at www.hospitalcompare.gov. Nevertheless, most investigations of hospitals that demonstrate efficient and effective care can reveal the proximate reasons for exemplary performance; likewise, through such studies hospitals can recognize opportunities for improvement. That is the power of electronic data: it can improve clinical processes based on clear evidence of what works and what does not.

Hospitals are most successful in improving quality when focusing on specific outcomes. For example, routine reporting of performance for the Trauma and Neurosurgery Service Lines at North Mississippi Medical Center, a 650-bed hospital in Tupelo, Mississippi, showed a higher than expected rate of complications and mortality.[11] In response, the hospital formed an interdisciplinary improvement team. Facilitating and enhancing patient-centered communication among interdisciplinary caregivers had a marked impact on improved outcomes within 12 months: resulting in a decrease of mortality (11.8 percent), morbidity (10 percent), complications (11.7 percent), and length of stay (2.8 days).

The interventions centered on collaboration and teamwork, which empowered all team members: nursing, physical therapy, occupational therapy, speech therapy, social work, respiratory therapy, nutrition, pharmacy, discharge planning, rehabilitation, home health, wound center, and pastoral care. They worked collaboratively to streamline care and reduce decision-to-action time by progressing the treatment plan as the patient condition permitted, rather than waiting for physician intervention. Expanding the learning of this team throughout the organization is just one example of the many reasons North Mississippi Medical Center has been nationally recognized for its quality patient care, receiving such distinctions as the 2006 Malcolm Baldrige National Quality Award.

Figure One: Identification of Five Performance Categories Based on CareScience Select Practice™

Using Data to Identify Effective Practices

Availability of structured clinical data can generate new knowledge about diagnostic or therapeutic interventions and provide scientific evidence of best practices. Information technology can turn large volumes of data into practical guides that can then be rapidly incorporated into clinical processes. The analysis of aggregated data can quickly identify gaps in evidence-based care and promote the rapid adoption of effective, efficient practices. This is the central tenet of the evidence-based medicine movement.

An early example of how the availability of structured clinical data can be used to facilitate the creation of an evidence-based approach is in the work done by Goldman and colleagues.[12] They constructed a computer protocol, based on personalized patient data, to determine which patients required admission to the coronary care unit due to the risk of acute myocardial infarction (AMI). They did this using aggregated clinical data on 1,379 patients with acute chest pain collected from two hospitals. The model protocol helped to clarify which signs and symptoms were important in predicting who was at risk for AMI and which were of little value. Use of the protocol reduced admissions to the unit by 11.5 percent without adversely affecting patients.

This example relied on data from only two hospitals. If clinical data were available in a structured format from a large number of hospitals, such data could assist researchers with similar types of studies and with determining which therapies are associated with the best outcomes—the essential feature of evidence-based medicine.

Other examples show how well-structured, aggregated data can be used to explore the relationship between practice patterns and clinical outcomes. Kerouac examined data on the relationship between adherence to clinical guidelines for patients requiring prolonged ventilation and clinical outcomes.[13] Data to examine these practices was collected from a collaboration among several academic medical centers that allowed an examination of 1,463 admissions to intensive care units. A wide variety in adherence to the guidelines was observed, and it was noted that two treatment practices, glycemic control and sedation practice, were specifically associated with better outcomes.

The clinicians noted above from North Mississippi Medical Center analyzed information derived from aggregated structured data to assess complication rates across patient populations within their institution. The analysis was possible due to availability of an algorithm that flagged potential complications using ICD-9 coded data. The institution also had a model that allowed comparisons to expected complication rates based on underlying patient characteristics. Through this process, the clinicians determined that the neurosurgical population was experiencing more complications than other patient populations, and that length of stay was increased beyond what would be expected given the underlying characteristics of the patients. A team of clinicians was able to uncover specific areas in need of process improvement; using this information, they were then able to implement targeted interventions. The result was better patient outcomes, higher staff satisfaction, and shorter lengths of stay.

Using Aggregate Data to Ensure Patient Safety

In 2000, with the publication of *To Err Is Human,* the IOM broke the silence surrounding medical errors and their consequences. The authors estimated that as many as 98,000 people die annually in American hospitals from medical errors. This number exceeds deaths from more highly publicized causes such as motor vehicle accidents, breast cancer, AIDS, or workplace injuries.[14]

The healthcare industry is a decade or more behind other high-risk industries in its attention to the careful examination of events leading to a medical mishap. Good reporting systems are an essential tool for gathering information about errors to prevent future occurrence. The IOM has recommended a nationwide mandatory reporting system for the collection of standardized information about adverse events that result in death or serious harm. Congress tasked the National Quality Forum with developing a core set of patient quality and safety standards to enable data aggregation, tracking, and analysis across institutions and states. In 2002, the National Quality Forum published a list of 27 serious reportable or "never" events, and in 2003 the organization endorsed a list of 30 evidence-based safe practices designed to prevent adverse events. (For a complete listing of "never events" and evidence-based safe practices, see the National Quality Forum website at http://www.qualityforum.org.)

AHRQ has developed a series of patient safety indicators using hospital inpatient administrative data. The patient safety indicators provide information about potential hospital complications, as well as adverse events following surgeries, procedures, and childbirth. They were developed after a comprehensive literature review, analysis of ICD-9-CM codes, evaluation by expert panels, empirical analyses, and risk adjustment. Patient safety indicators are free, publicly available, and can be used by hospitals to identify and analyze preventable adverse events and complications. AHRQ recognizes some weaknesses in these indicators and is now engaged in a systematic review and validation process by engaging with quality improvement and safety teams in hospitals around the country.

Voluntary reporting of both adverse events and so-called "near miss" events has been advocated as a method of facilitating root cause analysis and other types of investigations designed to prevent future mishaps. The ability to examine data on adverse or "near miss" events in a non-punitive environment can greatly facilitate the discovery of important safety concerns. Some institutions have shared de-identified, voluntarily reported data on "near misses" for learning purposes. By reporting near-miss transfusion errors anonymously, a group of 22 hospitals was able to pool experiences to learn about the conditions associated with "near misses" and the barriers that were used to prevent an adverse event. Such analyses will make future care safer for all involved.[15]

Using Aggregate Data to Improve Efficiency

In an efficient system, resources are used to get the best value for the money spent. Modern societies allocate a large portion of their wealth to the provision of healthcare services. The United States leads the world in health expenditures, as well as in efforts to study problems associated with quality and costs. Currently, healthcare spending in the United States accounts for some 16 percent of the gross national product, a staggering number that will continue to grow if substantial changes are not made. Policy debate has often focused on cost containment, as opposed to achieving the greatest value for the available resources. In 2005, Walker and his colleagues at the Center for Information Technology Leadership estimated that infrastructure changes, including standardized health information exchange among healthcare IT systems, could save $77.8 billion annually by maximizing the return on investments such as equipment, supplies, ideas, and energy.[16]

The combined understanding of well-structured, system-wide data and knowledge of evidence-based practices can have profound effects on clinical processes, outcomes, and efficiency. For example, St. Vincent Indianapolis Hospital utilizes a performance improvement tool that allows clinicians to analyze utilization of blood products and other resources.[17] By comparing utilization to evidence-based clinical guidelines, St. Vincent was able to understand where discrepancies occurred between actual practice and best practice. As St. Vincent is part of Ascension Health, a larger system of hospitals that utilizes the same system, it could compare its practice with other hospitals in the system and determine how blood resources could be used more efficiently while maintaining or improving patient care.

Through these systematic efforts, the organization reduced total blood use by 30 percent, decreased iatrogenic blood loss in critical care settings by 86 percent, and documented savings of $4.4 million in blood acquisition costs over five years. As this reduction was brought about by adherence to established guidelines for transfusions, these savings represent a clear reduction of waste (unnecessary transfusion). Moreover, patients were not subjected to the risk and discomfort of an unnecessary procedure. Total savings over five years were even larger. St. Vincent documented savings of $35 million over five years when labor, supplies, and the cost of adverse events that had been prevented due to the unnecessary administration of blood products were included. This is truly an example of how high-quality care is also efficient care, made possible because system-wide resource utilization data could be compared with data from peer institutions.

Universal Transparency and the Public's Right to Know

The IOM has recommended that the healthcare system provide information to patients and their families that allows them to make informed decisions when choosing among alternative treatments or selecting a health plan, hospital, or doctor. The information should describe a provider's performance related to safety, evidence-based practices, and patient satisfaction parameters.[18]

Meeting the IOM's recommendation requires universal transparency based on standardized performance metrics and outcomes reports that are easily accessible to everyone. Quality measurement and public reporting of performance metrics can be powerful mechanisms to drive improvements throughout the healthcare system. Both purchasers and consumer groups have embraced the notion of a transparent healthcare market where decision-making is supported by comparative information.

Fundamentally, individuals have a right to know this information and will be empowered with new knowledge. Providing reliable cost and quality information gives consumers more choice, creates incentives, and motivates the provision of better care for less money. According to the Department of Health and Human Services, improvements will come as providers see how their practice compares to others, and when consumer choice of healthcare providers is based on value.[19]

The first step in creating universal transparency is to develop standardized performance and outcome metrics. Some metrics exist today in Medicare and Medicaid databases, hospital discharge forms, and commercial claims databases. Although the data is primarily demographic and financial, it is almost always in an electronic format and can be easily aggregated for analysis. Unfortunately, many clinical data elements are neither standardized nor electronic, contained in paper charts that require tedious and costly manual abstraction. The National Committee for Quality Assurance (NCQA) estimates that failure to easily access and analyze clinical data is associated with "quality gaps" resulting in 37,600 to 81,000 deaths annually.[20]

Paying for Performance

The goals of a payment method should be to reward high-quality care and encourage the development of more effective ways of delivering care to maximize the value obtained for the resources expended.[21] Regrettably, financial barriers exist in American payment systems (both public and private) that do not facilitate systematic improvement. Fee-for-service payment systems are transaction-based models that reward the provision of providing an individual service. This model does not reward quality or efficiency; it simply reimburses caregivers for providing a service, regardless of its quality or outcome. Capitated systems reward efficiency in the provision of service ("episode efficiency") and the lowest-cost care over time. But they do not reward quality, patient outcomes, or patient-centered care. As a result, consumers, employers, and labor groups have called for a massive overhaul of public and private payment systems at all levels of care to reward the delivery of high-quality care and better outcomes.

In 2003, CMS launched a major demonstration project with 277 acute-care hospitals to publicly report evidence-based performance metrics and to provide monetary rewards to hospitals with the best outcomes. They targeted five common conditions: AMI, infarction, congestive heart failure, coronary artery bypass graft (CABG), community acquired pneumonia (CAP), and hip and knee replacement. After the first year of the demonstration, performance improved in all the hospitals and variation in performance narrowed.[22]

In 2004, CMS invited all hospitals participating in the Medicare and Medicaid programs to submit performance metrics for specific clinical conditions. It provided an incentive to hospitals willing to report the data and participate in government-sponsored quality improvement activities. In 2006 hospitals reported their results for 10 clinical measures and in 2007 surgical measures will be added to the list. This program has been very successful thus far, with approximately 4,200 hospitals currently participating.[23]

The CMS actions are in line with the larger industry trend toward "pay-for-performance" programs, and, according to the Leapfrog compendium, there are at least 100 pay-for-performance programs across the United States. Health plan giants such as Aetna, CIGNA, and Blue Cross and Blue Shield have already implemented incentive programs that reward providers for improvements in quality metrics, and organizations such as the Joint Commission and NCQA have begun to base accreditation decisions on performance metrics.

Conclusion

Americans are generally discriminating consumers, taking advantage of the wealth of information that exists on quality, safety, reliability, and price before making a major purchase. This has not occurred in healthcare because aggregate data comparing standard quality and safety metrics across multiple providers is not readily available. This has stemmed a national movement to create a uniform approach to quality measurement that can align stakeholder interests and inform value-based decisions. To fully realize this vision, data is key.

Work done by the IOM has focused national attention on the issue of quality and patient safety, as well as on the need for structured data systems for accurate measurement. And progress is being made. The Consumer-Purchaser Disclosure Project reported that healthcare data collection efforts now exist in 48 states and the District of Columbia.[24] Clinical measures are still the focus, although patient satisfaction metrics and structural measures, such as the implementation of electronic medical records, electronic prescribing, and the use of major patient registries, are also often rewarded. There is still considerable variation in the mix and weighting of measures, and this sometimes poses a barrier to widespread adoption. Although, according to AHRQ, the effectiveness of these metrics is mixed (direct payment to individuals is not always associated with improvements), states, hospitals, and health plans that publicly report performance metrics have begun to show improved outcomes.[25]

There is little doubt that well-structured data systems can bring about dramatic improvement in healthcare. From making performance transparent and driving evidence-based clinical processes to reducing medical errors to comparing costs, these actions cannot happen without the collection, aggregation, analysis, and dissemination of data. We must continue to work toward this future to meet the quality and safety goals set forth by the IOM and demanded by the public.

—⁓—

Beryl L. Vallejo, Dr.P.H., R.N., is the President of BJV Consulting, LLP in Englewood, Colorado, specializing in developing evidence-based, data-driven quality and performance improvement programs. Dr. Vallejo previously served as the Vice President of Quality, Safety and Outcomes Management at Centura Health in Colorado and as a Senior Consultant with CareScience, Inc. At Kelsey Research Foundation in Houston, Texas, Dr. Vallejo developed methodologies to evaluate quality improvements in the ambulatory care populations and disease state management programs. She served as a consultant to Joint Commission Resources for international accreditation and has extensive administrative and clinical experience as a chief nurse executive and clinical instructor. She received her B.S. in Nursing from Texas Woman's University and her master's and doctoral degrees from the University of Texas, School of Public Health, where she serves as an adjunct faculty member. She is a member of Sigma Theta Tau, American Association of Health Care Executives, National Association for Healthcare Quality, and the Health Care Coalition of Colorado.

Richard Bankowitz, M.D., M.B.A., F.A.C.P., is the Vice President and Medical Director for CareScience, where he is responsible for strategy, product delivery, consulting, sales, and advocacy efforts across the entire organization. Prior to joining CareScience in 2006, Dr. Bankowitz served as the Corporate Information Architect of the University HealthSystem Consortium (UHC). In his 12-year tenure with UHC, Dr. Bankowitz also held positions as Senior Director of Clinical Informatics, Director of Clinical Information Management, and Director of Clinical Evaluative Sciences. Dr. Bankowitz is board certified in the practice of Internal Medicine, is a Fellow of the American College of Physicians, and was a National Library of Medicine graduate trainee in medical informatics. He began his career at the University of Pittsburgh School of Medicine as an Assistant Professor of Medicine and Medical Informatics. Dr. Bankowitz is a graduate of the University of Chicago Pritzker School of Medicine and the University of Chicago Graduate School of Business.

Meg Horgan, R.N., M.S.N., is Vice President of Consulting and Customer Services at CareScience, and holds more than 20 years of experience in the healthcare quality area. In her role at CareScience, she leads consulting, education, and customer services. Ms. Horgan and her team guide healthcare leaders to approach today's complex quality issues through strategic planning, building effective care management processes and infrastructure, and providing the education, clinical analysis, and process redesign skills necessary to transform clinical performance. Her expertise in risk models enables healthcare organizations to not only interpret publicly reported performance but also to develop solutions to improve their quality measures. Prior to joining CareScience, Ms. Horgan was the Director of Clinical Redesign and Outcomes Management at Graduate Health Systems in Philadelphia. Prior to that she was the Administrator of the Quality Improvement Department at the Hospital of the University of Pennsylvania. She received her master's in Nursing and undergraduate degree from Gwynedd-Mercy College.

Eugene A. Kroch, Ph.D., is Vice President and Director of Research at CareScience. Dr. Kroch is also Lecturer in Health Care Systems in the Wharton School at the University of Pennsylvania, where he teaches health economics and econometrics. He is a Senior Fellow at the Leonard Davis Institute of Health Economics at the University of Pennsylvania, where he conducts research in the fields of econometrics, public policy, and health economics. He has served as a policy advisor for the U.S. Department of Health and Human Services, helping both the Office of the Coordinator for Health Information Technology and the Centers for Medicare and Medicaid Services. Dr. Kroch holds a B.S. degree in Economics from the Massachusetts Institute of Technology and M.A. and Ph.D. degrees in Economics from Harvard University, where he was a National Science Foundation Fellow.

—⟋⟍⟋—

[1] K. N. Lohr, ed., *Medicare: A Strategy for Quality Assurance* (Washington, D.C.: National Academy Press, 1990).

[2] A. Donabedian, *Explorations in Quality Assessment and Monitoring, Volume 1: The Definition of Quality and Approaches to Its Assessment* (Ann Arbor, MI: Health Administration Press, 1966).

[3] D. L. Sackett et al., *Evidence-based Medicine: How to Practice and Teach EBM* (New York: Churchill Livingstone, 1997).

[4] E. S. McGlynn et al., "The Quality of Health Delivered to Adults in the United States," *New England Journal of Medicine* 348 (2003): 2635–45.

[5] Williamson et al., *Medical Practice Information Demonstration Project: Final Report,* Office of the Assistant Secretary of Health, DHEW, Contract #282-77-0068GS (Baltimore, MD: Policy Research Inc., 1979); Institute of Medicine, *Assessing Medical Technologies* (Washington, D.C.: National Academy Press, 1985): 5; J. H. Ferguson, foreword to *Research on the Delivery of Medical Care Using Hospital Firms: Proceedings of a Workshop.* April 30 and May 1, 1990, Bethesda, MD. *Med Care* 1991; 29(7 Suppl):JS1-2 (July).

[6] Joseph M. Juran and Frank M. Gryna, *Quality Planning and Analysis: From Product Development Through Use, Third Edition,* (New York: McGraw-Hill Series in Industrial Engineering and Management Science, 1993).

[7] M. V. Pauly, D. J. Brailer, and E. A. Kroch, "Measuring Hospital Outcomes from a Buyer's Perspective," *American Journal of Medicine Quarterly* 11, no. 3 (1996): 112–22.

[8] D. J. Brailer, E. A. Kroch, and M. V. Pauly, "Comorbidity-Adjusted Complication Risk: A New Outcome Quality Measure," *Medical Care* 34, no. 5 (1996): 490–505.

[9] The public data includes the CMS MEDPAR file and all-payer data channeled through hospital associations in approximately 20 states. The latter makes up more than half of all hospital discharges in the United States. The private data comes from hospitals and health systems that subscribe to CareScience to guide their performance improvement efforts through quantitative analysis. CareScience models are calibrated on these data bases and are used to help hospitals better understand where they might improve quality and efficiency and how to achieve specific goals that are often related to targeted lines of service.

[10] Pauly et al., "Measuring Hospital Outcomes from a Buyer's Perspective."

[11] More information on North Mississippi Medical Center is available at http://www.carescience.com.

[12] L. Goldman et al., "A Computer Protocol to Predict Myocardial Infarction in Emergency Department Patients with Chest Pain," *New England Journal of Medicine* 318, no. 13 (1988): 797–803.

[13] M. A. Keroac et al., "The Relationship Between Evidence-Based Practices and Survival in Patients Requiring Prolonged Mechanical Ventilation in Academic Medical Centers," *American Journal of Medical Quality* 21, no. 2 (2006): 91–100.

[14] Institute of Medicine, Committee on Quality of Health Care in America, *To Err Is Human: Building a Safer Health System,* Linda T. Kohn, Janet M. Corrigan, and Molla S. Donaldson, eds. (Washington, D.C.: National Academy Press, 2000).

[15] H. S. Kaplan, "Getting the Right Blood to the Right Patient: The Contribution of Near-Miss Event Reporting and Barrier Analysis," *Transfusion Clinique et Biologique* 12, no. 5 (2005): 380–84.

[16] J. Walker et al., "The Value of Health Care Exchange and Interoperability," *Health Affairs* web exclusive, January 19, 2005. Available at

http://content.healthaffairs.org/cgi/content/full/hlthaff.w5.10/DC1 (accessed April 6, 2007).

[17] More information on St. Vincent Indianapolis Hospital can be found at http://www.carescience.com/.

[18] Institute of Medicine, Committee on Quality of Health Care in America, *Crossing the Quality Chasm: A New Health System for the 21st Century* (Washington, D.C.: National Academy Press, 2001).

[19] More information on HHS's value-based healthcare initiative is available at http://www.hhs.gov/transparency.

[20] National Committee for Quality Assurance, *State of Healthcare Quality 2006*. Available at http://www.ncqa.org.

[21] Institute of Medicine, *Crossing the Quality Chasm: A New Health System for the 21st Century*.

[22] *Premier Hospital Quality Incentive Demonstration White Paper for Year One*. Available at http://www.premierinc.com/quality-safety/tools/.

[23] "HQA Updates Hospital Compare Information," *AHA News*, March 20, 2006. Available at http//:www.ahanews.com.

[24] More information on the Consumer-Purchaser Disclosure Project is available at http://www.healthcaredisclosure.org.

[25] J. Hibbard, J. Stockard, and M. Trusler, "Does Publicizing Hospital Performance Stimulate Quality Improvement Efforts?" *Health Affairs* 22, no. 2 (2003): 84–94.

About the Editor

David Merritt is a project director at the Center for Health Transformation and the Gingrich Group. The Center, headed by former Speaker Newt Gingrich, is a collaboration of public and private sector leaders dedicated to transforming health and healthcare in America. Mr. Merritt advises Speaker Gingrich and leads the Center's projects on health information technology and expanding coverage to the uninsured.

He works extensively with congressional offices, the Bush administration, the media, and private sector leaders, particularly on the adoption of health information technology. He works closely with members of the Center on strategic planning and consulting. Mr. Merritt was appointed by Virginia governor Tim Kaine to serve on the governor's Health Information Technology Council, where he chairs the Business Case Subcommittee. He also serves on the Improving Quality, Consumer Awareness, and Prevention Workgroup of Governor Kaine's Health Reform Commission. He also serves on advisory boards to ICW, a German IT company, and the Center for Community Leadership, an initiative of Misys Healthcare Systems.

David Merritt's writing has been widely published, including in the *Chicago Tribune, Boston Globe, Chicago Sun-Times, Atlanta Journal-Constitution, Arizona Republic, Miami Herald,* and the *Washington Times.* Mr. Merritt is a frequent speaker with Center members, as well as with state and industry leaders, such as the Southern Governors Association and Citigroup. He is regularly quoted in trade and national press, and has been interviewed by the *New York Times, USA Today,* the *Wall Street Journal,* and ABC News.

Prior to joining the Center, he was with America's Health Insurance Plans, directing the association's educational programs with a primary focus on federal legislative and regulatory issues Mr. Merritt earned his master's degree in political science from Loyola University Chicago, with a primary focus on political theory and executive powers, and his bachelor's degree from Western Michigan University.

CHT Members Highlighted

Allscripts
America's Health Insurance Plans
American Academy of Family Physicians
American Hospital Association
American Medical Group Association
America's Health Insurance Plans
Blue Cross and Blue Shield Association
College of Health Information Management Executives (CHIME)
GE
General Motors
HealthTrio
Inland Northwest Health Services
Intermountain Healthcare
Microsoft
Misys Healthcare Systems
Siemens
UnitedHealth Group
WellPoint, Inc.

For more information on the Center for Health Transformation, its members, and its projects, please visit www.healthtransformation.net.